# HOW TEAMS TRIUMPH

# HOW TEAMS TRIUMPH

## MANAGING BY COMMITMENT

CLINTON M. PADGETT

**Forbes**Books

Published by ForbesBooks, Charleston, South Carolina.
Member of Advantage Media Group.

ForbesBooks is a registered trademark, and the ForbesBooks colophon is a trademark of Forbes Media, LLC.

Printed in the United States of America.

10  9  8  7  6  5  4  3  2  1

ISBN: 978-1-94663-330-9
LCCN: 2020914356

Cover design by Carly Blake.
Layout design by Wesley Strickland.

This custom publication is intended to provide accurate information and the opinions of the author in regard to the subject matter covered. It is sold with the understanding that the publisher, Advantage|ForbesBooks, is not engaged in rendering legal, financial, or professional services of any kind. If legal advice or other expert assistance is required, the reader is advised to seek the services of a competent professional.

Advantage Media Group is proud to be a part of the Tree Neutral® program. Tree Neutral offsets the number of trees consumed in the production and printing of this book by taking proactive steps such as planting trees in direct proportion to the number of trees used to print books. To learn more about Tree Neutral, please visit **www.treeneutral.com**.

Since 1917, Forbes has remained steadfast in its mission to serve as the defining voice of entrepreneurial capitalism. ForbesBooks, launched in 2016 through a partnership with Advantage Media Group, furthers that aim by helping business and thought leaders bring their stories, passion, and knowledge to the forefront in custom books. Opinions expressed by ForbesBooks authors are their own. To be considered for publication, please visit **www.forbesbooks.com**.

*This book is dedicated to the original developer of the Project Success Method, my friend and colleague, Dr. Tom Clark, who passed away in 2011.*

# CONTENTS

# ACKNOWLEDGMENTS

*FIRST, I WISH TO* recognize and thank the consultants of Project Success, Inc. that go out every day and bring order to chaos for our clients with their passion, diligence, and professionalism. I also wish to express my sincere thanks and gratitude to the thousands of clients who have engaged with PSI over the past thirty-seven-plus years to make their organizations better … particularly the senior leaders who had the foresight to realize things could be better, the vision to recognize that we could help, and the courage to implement the process. Together, these two groups form the most powerful of teams.

I want to thank my family for putting up with all the nights I spent in my office working on this book. I appreciate their patience with me and for allowing me the time necessary to complete it. Special thanks go out to my son, Hamilton, for asking me to play basketball or chess, and my daughter, Samantha, for asking me to read to her or play games with her, so that I would remember what's really important.

I would also like to thank my brother, Chris, for sharing the ride during our childhood—for sharing the blame when things inevitably went wrong and for putting up with the obligatory rites of passage visited on all younger brothers and for not hating me for them … eventually. Mostly I want to thank him for being able to make me laugh every single time we talk and for always having my back. A truer friend does not exist.

I am perhaps most thankful for the journey that inspired this book. While I will admit I didn't exactly volunteer to be an unpaid worker in my parents' entrepreneurial endeavors, the lessons learned and skills developed during that time paid immense dividends throughout my career and laid the foundation for the person I am today.

# THE PEOPLE SIDE OF PROJECT MANAGEMENT

**ONE DAY STEVE'S BOSS** walks into his office at Aeolus and says, "Congratulations, Steve. You're the project manager on the Fendhill Wind Farm Project." Steve's boss hands him a stack of documents, pats him on the back reassuringly, and leaves the room.

Steve stares at his boss's back as he leaves and then turns to the stack of papers. He shakes his head and thinks, "Not today. I've got five other top-priority projects with deliverables that are due in the next four weeks. This will have to wait."

A few weeks later, one of Steve's five projects is closing out, so he begins sifting through the Fendhill Wind Farm documents. It doesn't take long for him to break into a cold sweat. Steve has twenty-four months to deliver an incredibly complicated $100 million project. For each day he and his team are late, the contract calls for $1 million in liquidated damages. In addition to this, the Fendhill Wind Farm will be located in Spain, but Steve and many of his assigned project team are located at the Aeolus corporate headquarters in Florida or at satellite offices across the United States. This means that the people working on the project are spread out all over the world. It also means that Steve will have to work with two governments and suppliers from at least two countries to meet certain project specs. For example, 20 percent of the windmill components have to be produced in Europe, so Steve needs to make sure that his current approved supplier base meets these requirements; if not, the suppliers will need to be identified, negotiated with, and approved.

At Aeolus, there is no standard approved project management methodology in place, so everyone handles project management a little differently. It's unstructured and ad hoc, if it's done at all. There is no kickoff meeting where everyone who is working on the project flies to one central location—either in the United States or Spain—to discuss and plan the project. Instead, Steve's team of twenty-five—most of whom have never met each other—develops schedules and deadlines via email and phone. As Steve tries to make sense of the Fendhill Wind Farm and all of its moving parts, he is reminded, yet again, of the difficulty of running a project when he literally has no control over his team. Every single person Steve will be communicating with each week on behalf of the Fendhill Wind Farm Project works for someone else. Steve isn't their boss. He can't fire them. He can't hire them. He can't give them reviews. And while he can certainly schedule weekly project meetings with his team that he knows are vital to keep Fendhill on track, he cannot mandate their attendance. At this stage of the project, he's not sure whether they're even the right men or women for the job. Since he's not their boss, he doesn't know their skill sets, and he has no idea if any of them have worked on a project like this before. Not only do Steve's team members work for someone else, but several of the key personnel also work *in Spain*. This creates some additional issues. These team members speak a different language than Steve does, recognize different holidays than their American counterparts, have a different work style, and work within the parameters of different labor laws.

Steve knows he needs to get Fendhill moving, so he starts contacting his team, only to confirm his suspicions that Fendhill is one of five, six, or seven projects each team member is working on. So Steve not only doesn't have control of his team members, but he also has to compete with other projects for their time. And when Steve talks to his team members, they tell him the same thing: "Each one of my other project managers says their project is the most important. I'm doing the best I can." What Steve doesn't know is that some of his team members already resent him. They view project management as a punitive experience because every time they have been assigned to a project where "project management" was used, a project manager gave them unrealistic deadlines and expectations without having a conversation with them. Then the project manager used the "official schedule" to batter them when they missed a deadline that they had never committed to. Or worse, the project manager complained to their boss about their incompetence.

Suddenly, Steve feels buried by a crushing weight. How is he going to get such an incredibly complex wind farm project done successfully with all of these challenges? Plus, the twenty-four-month clock actually started when he was handed the project, so in reality he now has only twenty-three months to complete the project.

Twenty-five or thirty years ago, Steve never would have been in this predicament. Back then, project managers were powerful. They often had the ability to hire, fire, and promote their team members, and when someone didn't work out, five qualified people were chomping at the bit to fill the job. Today, project managers have little or no control over their teams. They can't hire, fire, or give pay raises, and when they lose a team member, they may not be given a resource with similar experience and skill sets to fill the lost position.

This shift has changed how we work. Several decades ago, a marketing project would have been run by and staffed by marketing personnel, an engineering project staffed by engineering personnel, and a software development project handled within the software group. Back then, projects were often planned and executed in silos. There was a marketing silo, an IT silo, and an engineering silo. That isn't the case anymore. Today, project work is cross-functional (it probably always should have been, but now the need is better recognized). Cross-functional project work means that a single project team may include people from engineering, testing, manufacturing, the shop floor, procurement, legal, human resources, and marketing.

Projects *should* be cross-functional. We should come out of our silos because doing so leads to better project results. Let's say that ACME Corporations is designing a new product. In my training classes, I always use the fictitious ACME Corporations for my product example—I love the old *Road Runner* cartoons—so I'll use it here too. Interestingly, the coyote always failed in his attempts to catch the road runner for many of the same reasons our projects fail—poor planning, improper equipment, faulty execution. In this example, the ACME Corporation's marketing team created marketing plans and marketing collateral to sell the product without having had a conversation with engineering on the viability of the product design or with manufacturing to understand their challenges. Everyone developed their piece of the project in their respective silos.

Here is what should have happened instead. Marketing, engineering, and manufacturing should have come together face-to-face, along with any other needed functions, and built a plan that all agreed to. Engineering would then have been able to design and test product functions that the customer wanted and that marketing would have been able to sell. Manufacturing would have then ensured that the design was optimized for manufacturability and the like. This is a very different scenario with a much higher probability of success.

The challenge with cross-functional teamwork is that it's created a matrix environment for project managers like Steve. In this environment, each cross-functional team member officially reports to someone other than the project manager, usually their functional manager. Whoever the team member works for full-time has both the whip and the carrot because they can hire, fire, give pay raises, and even promote that person. The project manager cannot. As we saw with Steve and the Fendhill project, in a matrix environment, each team member simultaneously works on many projects that have nothing to do with the project Steve needs done. Steve gives the team member direction on only *one* project—his own.

## EXAMPLE MATRIX ORGANIZATIONAL CHART

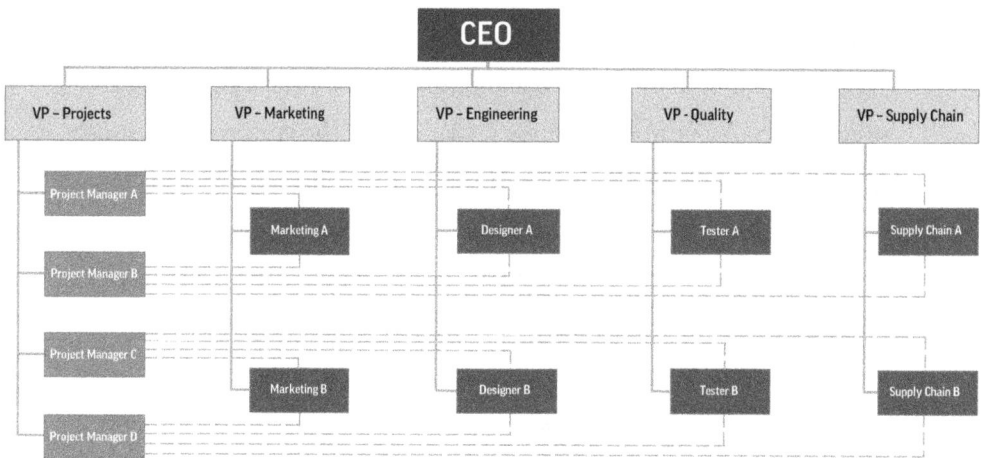

In a matrix environment, project managers have little to no control over their resources. They don't have the whip, so they can't come down on team members for failing to do a good job, and they don't have the carrot, so they can't reward them for doing well. In reality, project managers don't have the ability to *make* the people who are assigned to their project do anything. So how do today's project managers deliver a quality project on time and on budget in a matrix? By leveraging their people skills. Today's successful project managers know how to build loyalty and trust among their project teams so that those teams want to help them achieve a goal. The challenge is that many project managers tend to be strong on technical skills but weak on relationship building.

In 2009 I published *The Project Success Method: A Proven Approach for Achieving Superior Project Performance in as Little as Five Days.* That book clearly explains the Project Success Method, which is the process that my company, Project Success Incorporated (PSI), and hundreds of our clients use to effectively manage projects around the globe. While *The Project Success Method* has been a well-received guide for the technical side of project management and is even used in some college courses, it does not comprehensively address the people side of the equation. As a project manager, you can be the smartest and most technically sound person in the room, but in a matrix environment, if you don't have the leadership skills required to effectively motivate people, your project will fail by going over budget, missing agreed-upon deadlines, or delivering poor quality.

In *How Teams Triumph*, I reinforce and build on where *The Project Success Method* leaves off and show you how to plug the gap between the technical expertise needed to design a project and the softer skill set—the people skills—needed to get your team excited about and committed to finishing a quality project on time and on budget.

At PSI we have already shown hundreds of companies how to do this. After one of our northern California Fortune 500 clients started using the Project Success Method (PSM), they reduced their project lateness by 90 percent while also reducing cycle time. That's a huge improvement, especially considering the fact that these projects can require up to twenty, thirty, or even forty team members. Imagine how much finishing a project eight months earlier than expected saves on personnel costs alone. By the way, did I mention the reduction in cycle time they were able to achieve? This company has mastered the Project Success Method in its entirety, both the process *and* people skills needed to excel at project management in the twenty-first century. In this book I'm going to show you how to do the same.

## THE IMPORTANCE OF TEAMWORK

I'm a huge college football fan and a Georgia Tech alumnus, so whenever Georgia Tech has a home football game, you'll find me in the stands. In the middle of the 2017 football season, I was sitting with one of my good friends—fellow South Carolinian and fellow proud alumnus Joe Hamilton—watching Georgia Tech get its backside kicked (again) by the University of Georgia. Joe is a fantastic guy with a greater-than-average understanding of how successful teams work. He's a former Georgia Tech quarterback; he earned first-team All American honors, won the Davey O'Brien Award for best NCAA quarterback, and was the first runner-up for the Heisman Trophy. While we watched the game, instead of talking about the score, Joe and I couldn't stop talking about the people on the field and sideline. Our team was passionless. Their bodies were there, but their minds were somewhere else. They didn't jump up and down after plays, they didn't motivate each other to do better, and they didn't communicate. No wonder we were losing!

Whether you're playing football, designing a new product, or managing a project, teamwork is everything. It holds sports teams together—how often have we heard that a head coach lost his job because he "lost the locker room," meaning that his team was no longer working as a team and no longer respected his authority. Teamwork also holds relationships together, and it holds projects together. This is why I personally view life in terms of "we." If Georgia Tech is losing, we are losing. If one of my clients is struggling with project management, we are struggling. This *we* attitude is crucial to effective project management.

Looking back, I realize I've been part of teams my entire life. I grew up in Orangeburg, South Carolina—a small town with a population of less than fourteen thousand. My upbringing was unconventional to say the least, in large part because of my dad, who was a serial entrepreneur that expected his kids to work on his team. When I was growing up, Dad owned gas stations, beer and wine stores, and a liquor store, among other businesses. Not to be left out, my mom owned a wine and cheese shop. When I was six years old, I was picking up trash in the parking lot. By the time I was eight years old, I worked at my dad's gas stations pumping gas for customers. I wasn't tall enough to check the oil, but I could wash windshields, so I did that too. From a very young age, I was a team player. I worked with my dad, my mom, my brother, and my dad's employees to make our customers happy. That was our common goal, and each of us had our own role in contributing to that goal. This is exactly how project management should work.

Working for my dad gave me a sense of being part of a team and probably helped develop my love of numbers. Back then, we didn't have electronic cash registers, so I wore one of those metal devices that clips onto your belt and has cylinders for quarters, nickels, dimes, and pennies. I would total our customers' bills and make change from that belt. At the beer and wine and liquor stores, I'd carry beer cases to the customers' cars. At the drive-up window, I'd sell them their requested products, calculate and add the 4 percent sales tax, take their money, and calculate the change in my head. I saw people from all walks of life and of every economic status come through our businesses. One day I'd say hello to the town mayor as I pumped his gas; the next day I'd be talking with a panhandler while ringing up his Coke and peanuts (a combination that is considered a Southern delicacy). My dad always treated both with the same level of respect. His saying was, "Money is green. It spends no matter who hands it to you," which I interpreted to mean that all people have value regardless of their occupation. That's an attitude I've taken my whole life—no matter their perceived station in life, all people matter. Being exposed to every class of people taught me how to deal with people as individuals, another crucial skill for project management.

At eighteen, I didn't really know what I wanted to do with my life, so I joined the US Navy and spent almost five years of my six-year enlistment on an aircraft carrier, the USS *America* (CV-66) as an electrician's mate. When I first arrived aboard the ship, I was twenty years old but looked sixteen. A senior enlisted man took pity on me and said, "Son, you look lost. Let me help you out. Here are some things you need to come to terms with, and if you do, your time on board will go much more smoothly and be a lot less stressful." First, he explained the term *haze gray and underway*, which was the color the ship was painted and where we were expected to be at all times. Then he quoted the phrase "Sailors are made for ships, and ships are made for sea." This was the navy's way of explaining that its mission was best achieved by being at sea all the time. Finally he said (and this was my personal favorite), "Being in the navy is just like being in prison." He smiled, paused for effect, and continued. "With the added risk of drowning." At that moment, I truly realized what I'd gotten myself into when I signed up for a six-year enlistment—a job you could never quit, but if you were fired from, your long-term employability would be limited. Lesson learned!

Navy days were long (twelve to sixteen hours a day, seven days a week) and 100 percent focused on team and commitment. Every one of us worked toward a common goal by performing the job they were assigned. If a single person failed at their assigned task, the overall mission could be compromised.

After six years in the navy, I was ready for a change, so I left to work in a shipyard. That's where I got my first lesson in thermodynamics. I walked into the shipyard, which was obviously right on the water, and the winds coming off the water sliced right through me. It was frigid. I remember lying in the bilge at the bottom of the ship where I was running electrical cables, realizing that the heat from my body was radiating through the hull into the ocean. That was the lesson in thermodynamics: My body wasn't a big enough heat sink, and it was causing me to freeze. I vividly recall thinking, "There must be something better to do with my life than this." That's when I decided that college wasn't such a bad idea. So I applied to and was lucky enough to get accepted into the Georgia Institute of Technology (Georgia Tech) to study engineering. After all, I'd wanted to be an engineer since I was nine or ten years old.

College was my next lesson in working as a team. First, I received my electrical engineering degree from Georgia Tech, and then I later earned my MBA from Duke University. At both schools, I had to work on teams with other students. Sometimes, as with all teams, there were issues. Someone wouldn't do their work on time, or they'd get lazy with the project, and other team members would have to pick up the slack so we wouldn't get a bad grade. If you think about it, most of us have early memories of teamwork, even if forced, in school projects, playing sports, or jobs. The thing about teamwork is that it doesn't work if the players on that team can't (or won't) communicate, aren't committed to each other, or don't understand how their role in the team affects the common goal. Nowhere is this more obvious than when your favorite college football team is losing but can't seem to muster enough enthusiasm to care.

## PEOPLE SKILLS MATTER

As I already mentioned, I have wanted to be an electrical engineer for as long as I can remember. When I was only ten or eleven, I would ride my bicycle to one of our two nearby colleges to check out books on robotics and lasers. In fact, one of my science projects in high school was to use a laser to create a hologram (yes, this was shortly after the original *Star Wars* was released). So, while I've always been interested in the technical side of engineering, I didn't realize how much the people side was ignored in technical fields like engineering until I went to college. At Georgia Tech, I studied hard. I opened and closed the library Sunday through Friday. Saturday was reserved for watching Georgia Tech sports or having fun (I was a singing bartender for a while, which is hands down the most fun job I've ever had, but that's a different story for another book). As I said, I opened and closed the library six days a week. My attitude was that you might be smarter than me, but you are *not* going to outwork me. However, I noticed that no matter how hard I studied, some students got better grades than I did. This bothered me until I realized they never got dates.

Suddenly, I was OK with my place in the pecking order. I had better people skills and, as it turns out, social skills matter!

When I got out into the real world and started working, it became even more obvious to me that many engineers lacked the social skills necessary for teamwork. This is because we engineers often live in a very black-and-white world. I like this about the engineering field. I've always liked looking at the answer key in the back of the book and confirming that two plus two is indeed four. I don't like subjective questions.

I remember having to write an essay about *The Great Gatsby* for an English literature exam in high school. The assignment read "Please describe the significance of the author's use of the color red in *The Great Gatsby*." Years later I still don't know what the correct answer was; however, I can tell you it definitely was not "Red is the author's favorite color." I had not read the book, and it was the best answer I could come up with at sixteen years of age. I learned two things from that experience: First, I should have followed the assignment and read the book. Second, and more importantly, I learned that I dislike subjective questions. Even if I had been able to interview F. Scott Fitzgerald about his use of red, my answer might have been wrong. Why? Because the question wasn't really "Please describe the significance of the author's use of the color red in *The Great Gatsby*." The real question was "Please describe what your teacher believes the significance of the author's use of the color red is in *The Great Gatsby*." Those are two very different questions!

I like objective answers, and I bet that most people who walk into a building or cross a bridge also like to know that the engineers who built those structures don't like subjectivity. They like precision. This attitude is all well and good when designing and building structures, but a black-and-white attitude is antithetical to teamwork. I've watched engineers bring this attitude to teams. It's a black-and-white "you're wrong; I'm right" or "you lose; I win" mentality. On a good team, no one person wins or loses. The team wins or loses. The team works together collaboratively to develop a solution that works.

## THE PEOPLE SIDE OF PSI

For the last twenty-five-plus years, my job has been to help technical-minded people learn how to develop teams that can deliver massive projects, which often last several years, on time, on budget, and of high quality.

My company works with global corporations, such as Caterpillar, Inc., the Coca-Cola Company, CNN, AGCO, Maxim Integrated, and Marvell Technology Group (to name a few), across all industries to plan and execute their largest projects. We do this by training project teams in the Project Success Method and then working with them to ensure they have the skills to take over the project as we work ourselves out of a job. The Project Success Method was developed by Dr. Tom Clark. It's based on the Critical Path Method from the 1950s, with an added emphasis on the people side of project management. It's a project management process that allows the project team members to identify their own actionable items, ones that need to be done to complete the project. This results in more accurate project timelines leading to high-quality projects that are finished on time and on budget. The Project Success Method also clarifies roles and expectations for each team member, documents project plans and schedules, makes team members accountable for their work, and improves communication. PSI has helped companies develop and launch new products ranging from agricultural tractors to semiconductor chips; plan sponsor activations for major events such as the Olympics, the

FIFA World Cup, and the UEFA EURO; develop and implement new software; and successfully complete mergers and acquisitions, just to name a few, using the Project Success Method. Additionally, PSI has helped firms execute major construction projects such as the design and construction of 1 World Trade Center, the tallest building in the Western Hemisphere and seventh tallest in the world, as well as the design and construction of New York City's Bank of America Tower—the fifth tallest building in that city and the first skyscraper to receive a platinum LEED certification for green design[1]—and the north and south towers of the Time Warner Center, both of which are among the fifty tallest buildings in New York City.

At PSI our driving goal is to make you fully self-sufficient at implementing the Project Success Method as quickly as possible. This knowledge transfer starts with teaching the Project Success Method. Two-day training sessions get everyone who is part of the project team in a room so they can learn how to *work together* to successfully plan future projects. I really love the way one of our clients describes the value we add. He says, "Other courses might teach you how to use a hammer, a drill, or a screwdriver—the individual tools you need to use to build something. But, while you learn how to use the tools, you don't gain the knowledge needed to actually build anything. With the Project Success Method, I learn how to build a table. Along the way, of course, I also learn how to use each tool *while building the table.* So when I leave the training, not only can I use the tools, but I can also build tables. Plus, I can then extrapolate from that knowledge so I can build chairs, stools, etc."

---

1    Jeff Desjardins, "The 100 Tallest Buildings in New York City," Visual Capitalist, April 26, 2019, https://www.visualcapitalist.com/100-tallest-buildings-in-new-york-city/.

When I first started at PSI in 1994, I focused more on process than people. Luckily, the process protects the people on the team, so I was safe in doing so. However, the more I used the Project Success Method and the more I taught others to use it, the more I came to understand *why* the process specified certain things. For instance, one rule is that we can only have a single person assigned to a task as the owner, and that person must be physically present, and that person must verbally agree to accept the role. I came to see that learning about the people side of things led to great results, in the same way that learning to use a hammer and saw led to the creation of a table or chair. PSI focuses on developing teams that will build that table. We know that when you work in a matrix—when you have team members all over the world whom you have no direct authority over—developing a relationship with them is as important to getting the project done as is understanding each action that must be taken to complete the project.

While the people side is crucial to project success, it takes a while for some to wrap their head around that fact. Several years ago, I was teaching a class in Irvine, California, when I was introduced to someone at Warner Brothers who was interested in how we might be able to help him streamline his process and how our techniques could be applied to movie production. As is the case with any large project, if a movie goes over deadline, it costs money. So I drove to Los Angeles from Irvine and met with this vice president over lunch. He was polished, engaged, and clearly used to running the show. Once I started talking about PSI and our process, he stopped eating, raised his eyebrow, and said, "Wait a minute, I thought you said you were an engineer. What is all this touchy-feely people stuff?" He had probably expected me to tell him, "Do this; don't do that; this will work here; this won't" and leave it at that. He had expected me to focus more on the process used than on the people involved. It dawned on me then that, yeah, the touchy-feely stuff is exactly what we're talking about. Project management isn't just about math and process. It's also about people.

At PSI, we have always done just three things.

- We teach people how to manage projects using the repeatable, team-centric Project Success Method—a proven, collaborative approach that enables teams to build actionable project plans that they are committed to delivering.

- We help our clients complete their projects successfully by taking the knowledge learned in the classroom and implementing it on the client's actual projects. We stand beside the person who becomes the project manager, mentoring that person, teaching them everything we know over the course of that project so that when it is over they can manage future projects on their own.

- We provide guidance in the development and implementation of effective Project Success Systems including the selection and implementation of project management software, project procedures documentation, report formats, and status memo standards.

Essentially our mission is twofold: to bring order out of chaos and to work ourselves out of a job.

## WHAT YOU WILL LEARN IN THIS BOOK

In *How Teams Triumph*, you will learn the people skills necessary to implement the Project Success Method with your cross-functional, matrixed project team:

- How to use the tools in your tool kit to develop a strong, communicative, committed team

- How to gather the right team

- How to foster accountability by developing relationships that ensure people matter

- How to prepare for and deal with unknowns

- How to effectively use your team to exercise project control

- How to support your team without micromanaging

- How to communicate most effectively with your team

- How to manage dispute resolution

- How to work with teams operating internationally or virtually

I have the greatest job in the world because I know that if I follow my process and use my people skills to build teams, I will be successful in any project that I work on. Each one is unique, but I know going in that I'm going to win and that the rest of the team will win too. It's like a baseball player walking up to the plate knowing he's going to get a hit. The pitcher is always different, and so are the ballpark and the uniforms, but the outcome is the same. You will always triumph if you follow our process and rally your team behind you.

"Two things are necessary
for great achievement: a plan,
and not quite enough time."

—LEONARD BERNSTEIN

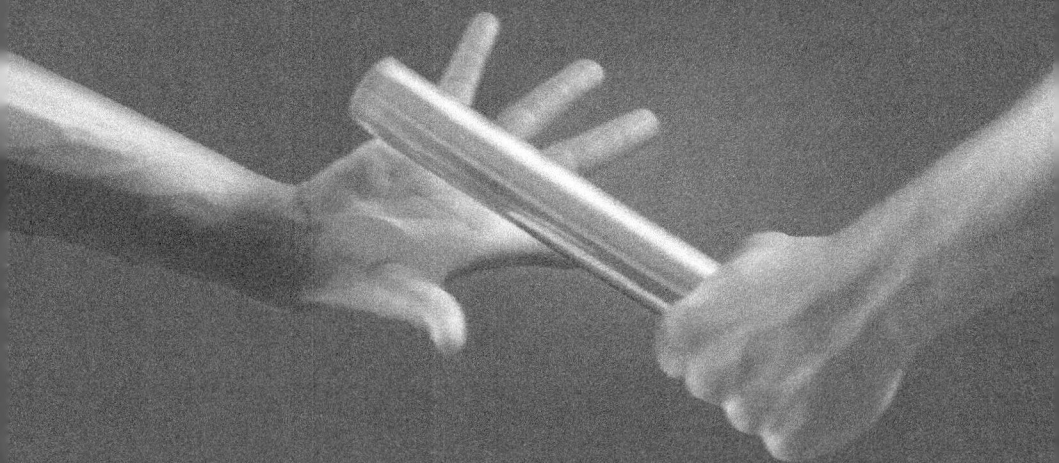

# THE PROJECT SUCCESS METHOD

*PROJECT MANAGEMENT IS* all about people and process. While *How Teams Triumph* focuses on the importance of people, project managers must have a basic understanding of PSI's Project Success Method to understand how people and process work together.

The Project Success Method process works like this. A company engages PSI to mentor its team members in project management. First, we get everyone who will be working on that project in a room for two days. The goal is for them to learn a proven, actionable, collaborative methodology with a common vocabulary, so we are all on the same page, speaking the same language. This common vocabulary is vital because confusion is one of the enemies of successful project completion. For example, if I were to ask a group of ten people to define a "critical activity," I would probably get three or four different definitions.

One person would say, "A critical activity is one that is very important to my boss, so it's critical to my career advancement that I get it done."

Another might say, "A critical activity is one that is on the critical list, meaning it's in trouble and needs attention."

A third person might say, "A critical activity is something on the critical path of the project, which means if it's late by a day, the project is late by a day. If we can deliver that task one day early, we'll finish the project one day early."

The third person's definition is correct, by the way. But can you see how easily miscommunication happens when a common language is not established? Can you imagine the frustration a team member working on multiple projects would feel trying to keep track of which definition each project manager uses? It would be a nightmare, hence our need to be consistent in our definitions.

After the training, the team comes to an agreement on the direction of the project. In other words, they decide what's in the project's scope and what's out of the project's scope, followed by customer feedback, alignment, and agreement. This information is formalized in a written document called a project charter, a document that clearly defines the requirements of the project so that everyone involved in the project—every stakeholder—knows and agrees to the direction in which the project is heading.

## TYPICAL TIMELINE FOR INITIAL PLANNING SESSION

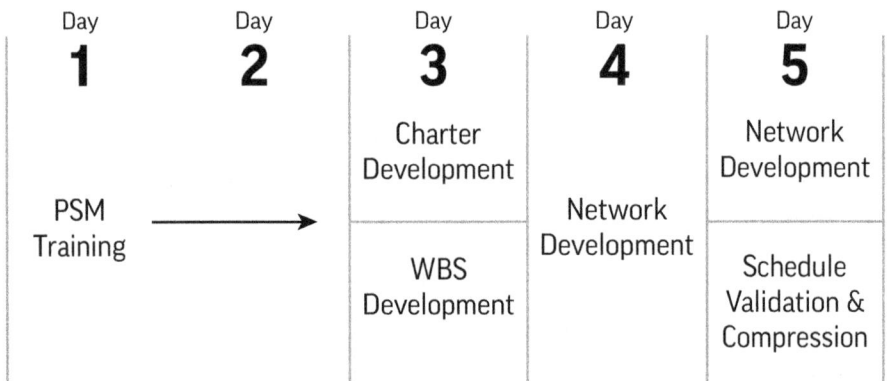

| Day 1 | Day 2 | Day 3 | Day 4 | Day 5 |
|---|---|---|---|---|
| | | Charter Development | | Network Development |
| PSM Training | ⟶ | | Network Development | |
| | | WBS Development | | Schedule Validation & Compression |

After the charter is written and approved, we establish the work breakdown structure. This means that we identify the activities that need to be completed to finish the project. This may include a few hundred activities or, possibly, several thousand. Often activities we are unaware of during the planning stage will need to be added later on. Of course, we don't plan every hour of every day. Instead, for these near-term activities, we recommend creating tasks that take between five and ten working days. Activities that are unclear to us because they are set to take place far in the future can be identified in less detail (durations longer than ten days). This is how we strike a balance between not drowning in details and establishing manageable pieces of work.

Below is a sample work breakdown structure.

## PARTIAL EXAMPLE WBS
### (Pyramid Format)

**Century Manufacturing Company**
**Athens Plan Silver Anniversary Celebration**
**(St. James)**

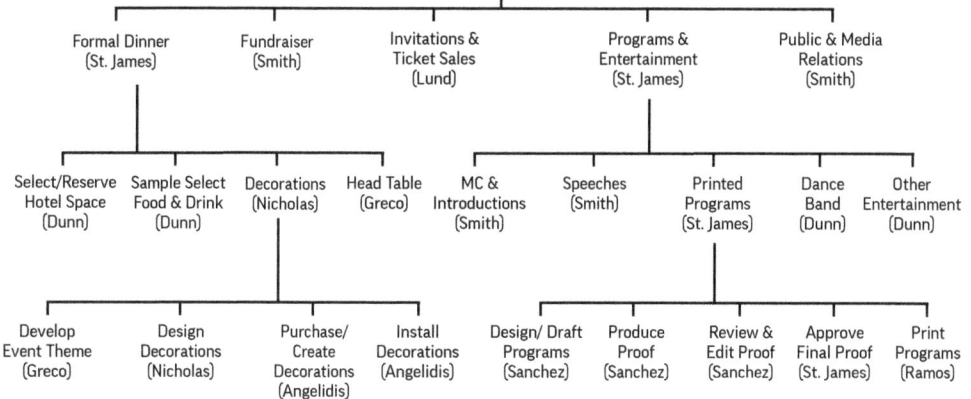

| Formal Dinner (St. James) | Fundraiser (Smith) | Invitations & Ticket Sales (Lund) | Programs & Entertainment (St. James) | Public & Media Relations (Smith) |

| Select/Reserve Hotel Space (Dunn) | Sample Select Food & Drink (Dunn) | Decorations (Nicholas) | Head Table (Greco) | MC & Introductions (Smith) | Speeches (Smith) | Printed Programs (St. James) | Dance Band (Dunn) | Other Entertainment (Dunn) |

| Develop Event Theme (Greco) | Design Decorations (Nicholas) | Purchase/ Create Decorations (Angelidis) | Install Decorations (Angelidis) | Design/ Draft Programs (Sanchez) | Produce Proof (Sanchez) | Review & Edit Proof (Sanchez) | Approve Final Proof (St. James) | Print Programs (Ramos) |

Then we begin to build a model of the project. This is often referred to as the network diagram, which is a sequence of activities connected with arrows that establish the order of events.

## Predecessor                    Successor

| Activity A | **THEN** → | Activity B |

Activity A finishes then Activity B can start

We start the network diagram process by sequencing the activities identified in the work breakdown structure. This is accomplished by asking two very simple questions:

1.  Given where we are in the project, what activity or activities *can* I perform next?
2.  What activity or activities *have to be* completed before this task can start?

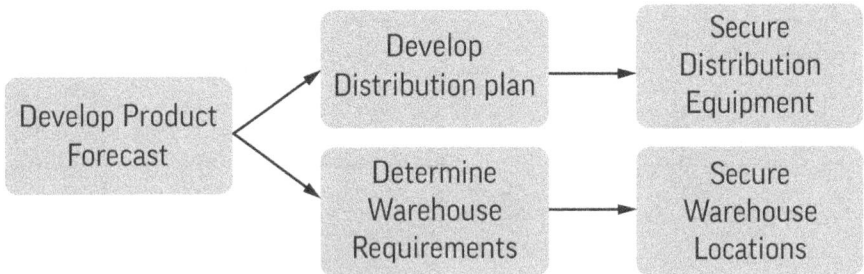

This simple network shows that we must develop a product forecast before developing a distribution plan. Once the distribution plan is developed, we can secure the distribution equipment. Think of this sequencing like building a house. You can't put the roof on until after you have erected the walls. There's a sequenced order that you must follow to complete the project.

Next, we identify a task owner or activity manager for each activity. It's important here to understand what role an activity manager plays. The activity manager is the person on the team who has agreed to take responsibility for and ownership of a task to make sure it gets done. The resource is the person who physically does the labor. The activity manager doesn't necessarily do the work personally but does make sure that the work gets done, and it's their reputation on the line if it doesn't. We then work with each activity manager to understand how long each activity will take. The length of each activity is called a duration. Of course, the duration is affected by each team member's experience and availability.

Once we've identified durations for each activity, we calculate the critical path, which is the sequence of activities that determines the project completion date. This is accomplished by looking at every single series of activities (path) that must be finished to complete a project—studying the way they're organized or sequenced (what happens first, second, and third, and what happens in parallel) along with their associated durations—and identifying the path(s) that takes the longest. These are the activities that absolutely must be done as scheduled for the project to be completed on time. Not all activities will make it onto this list, and that's a really good thing, a point I'll talk about later.

In this final step, we compress the schedule in order to reach the project deadline. We accomplish this by focusing on the critical path and making changes that save time on the project. For most projects, this means getting rid of some activities or adding resources. We may need to operate some tasks in parallel that we would have preferred to conduct in a series. We may need to change our technical approach to some tasks or start the project earlier than planned. In some cases, a reduction in scope may be necessary. This is also the ideal time to determine whether the project is unavailable and should be canceled.

Here's a simple example called the Melbourne Plant Development project. This project required leasing a building with ten-thousand-square-meters of production, warehouse, and office space; installing ten equipment cells; and procuring materials for the first month of production, as well as hiring and training thirty employees. The work breakdown structure identified twenty-one activities, which we've networked below.

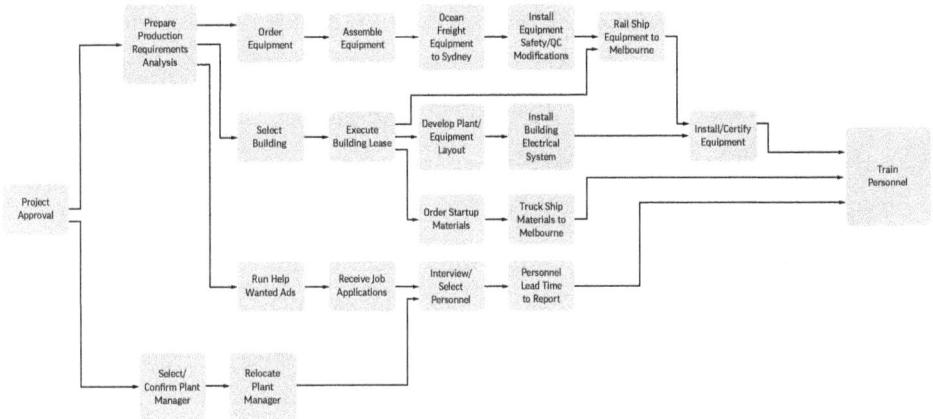

After assigning activity managers and working through durations for each activity, we were able to identify a critical path (the shaded activities in the Century Manufacturing Company Melbourne Plant Development network diagram on the next page). It is important to note that this date is not necessarily the deadline for the project. It is how long the project, as currently planned, will take to finish.

## CENTURY MANUFACTURING COMPANY
### Melbourne Plant Development

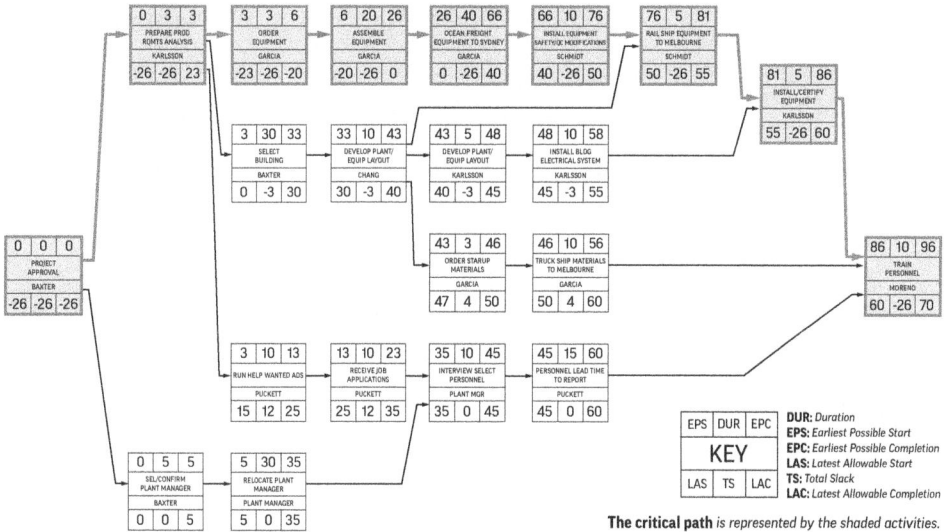

**Network diagram nodes (EPS | DUR | EPC / name / resource / LAS | TS | LAC):**

- 0 | 3 | 3 — PREPARE PROD RQMTS ANALYSIS — KARLSSON — -26 | -26 | 23
- 3 | 3 | 6 — ORDER EQUIPMENT — GARCIA — -23 | -26 | -20
- 6 | 20 | 26 — ASSEMBLE EQUIPMENT — GARCIA — -20 | -26 | 0
- 26 | 40 | 66 — OCEAN FREIGHT EQUIPMENT TO SYDNEY — GARCIA — 0 | -26 | 40
- 66 | 10 | 76 — INSTALL EQUIPMENT SAFETY/OSC MODIFICATIONS — SCHMIDT — 40 | -26 | 50
- 76 | 5 | 81 — RAIL SHIP EQUIPMENT TO MELBOURNE — SCHMIDT — 50 | -26 | 55
- 81 | 5 | 86 — INSTALL/CERTIFY EQUIPMENT — KARLSSON — 55 | -26 | 60

- 3 | 30 | 33 — SELECT BUILDING — BAXTER — 0 | -3 | 30
- 33 | 10 | 43 — DEVELOP PLANT/ EQUIP LAYOUT — CHANG — 30 | -3 | 40
- 43 | 5 | 48 — DEVELOP PLANT/ EQUIP LAYOUT — KARLSSON — 40 | -3 | 45
- 48 | 10 | 58 — INSTALL BLDG ELECTRICAL SYSTEM — KARLSSON — 45 | -3 | 55

- 0 | 0 | 0 — PROJECT APPROVAL — BAXTER — -26 | -26 | -26

- 43 | 3 | 46 — ORDER STARTUP MATERIALS — GARCIA — 47 | 4 | 50
- 46 | 10 | 56 — TRUCK SHIP MATERIALS TO MELBOURNE — GARCIA — 50 | 4 | 60
- 86 | 10 | 96 — TRAIN PERSONNEL — MORENO — 60 | -26 | 70

- 3 | 10 | 13 — RUN HELP WANTED ADS — PUCKETT — 15 | 12 | 25
- 13 | 10 | 23 — RECEIVE JOB APPLICATIONS — PUCKETT — 25 | 12 | 35
- 35 | 10 | 45 — INTERVIEW SELECT PERSONNEL — PLANT MGR — 35 | 0 | 45
- 45 | 15 | 60 — PERSONNEL LEAD TIME TO REPORT — PUCKETT — 45 | 0 | 60

- 0 | 5 | 5 — SEL/CONFIRM PLANT MANAGER — BAXTER — 0 | 0 | 5
- 5 | 30 | 35 — RELOCATE PLANT MANAGER — PLANT MANAGER — 5 | 0 | 35

**KEY**

| EPS | DUR | EPC | DUR: Duration |
|---|---|---|---|
| | KEY | | EPS: Earliest Possible Start / EPC: Earliest Possible Completion / LAS: Latest Allowable Start |
| LAS | TS | LAC | TS: Total Slack / LAC: Latest Allowable Completion |

**The critical path** is represented by the shaded activities.

Finally, we compressed our schedule in order to reach the project deadline. With the Melbourne project, our starting point for compression was ninety-six workdays (as indicated in the upper righthand corner of the "train personnel" task). However, we had a deadline of seventy working days (seen in the lower righthand corner of the task), so once we started the compression process, we knew we needed to reduce the overall project duration by twenty-six working days to hit our deadline (96-70=26). Working together as a team, the activity managers for the critical path activities continued to make changes, looking at the resulting critical path after each change until our schedule met the deadline.

---

"Planning is bringing the future into the present so that you can do something about it now."

—Alan Lakein

---

This is what happens during a typical planning session, which can take anywhere from a couple of days to a couple of weeks depending on project size and complexity. Following the planning session, the project manager hosts update and control meetings. These frequent meetings are designed to make sure the team members are completing their tasks, particularly those on the critical path, as scheduled. They also give the project manager and team members an opportunity to make the course corrections (add/delete tasks, change durations, change the sequence, etc.) needed to have the plan reflect what is actually happening on the project. Finally, these weekly or biweekly update and control meetings allow us to address any project slippages, which occurs when a critical path activity takes longer than originally anticipated to be completed.

For more details about the Project Success Method, read *The Project Success Method: A Proven Approach for Achieving Superior Project Performance in as Little as Five Days.*

---

"It is the long history of humankind (and animal kind, too) that those who learned to collaborate and improvise most effectively have prevailed."

—Charles Darwin

---

# CHAPTER 1 KEY TAKEAWAYS

- The team needs to have a common, consistent approach to project management.

- Establish a precise and consistent project management vocabulary.

- Identify a task owner or activity manager for each activity.

- Calculate the critical path, the sequence of activities that determines the project completion date.

- Compress the schedule in order to reach the project deadline.

- Conduct regular update and control meetings to: make sure the team members complete the critical path activities on schedule; give team members an opportunity to change durations; and allow the team to account for, and address, schedule slippage.

"There can only be one most important thing. Many things may be important, but only one can be most important."

—ROSS GARBER

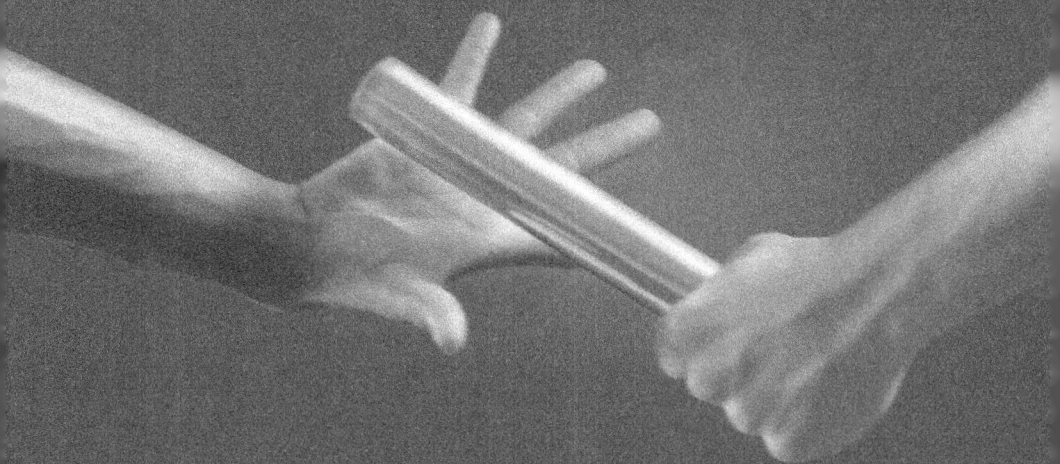

# CHAPTER 2:

# WHY DO PROJECTS FAIL?

*IN 1990, I WORKED* for the Coca-Cola Company in Atlanta as a sales equipment engineer. During this time, we were running a campaign known as "Magic Summer '90." Part of this campaign involved Coca-Cola cans that contained cash or prizes instead of soda. Of course, Coca-Cola didn't want its customers to know which cans had the prizes, so the engineers needed to develop a can that could contain and deliver the prize but still feel like a regular can of Coke. The result was called MagiCan. The can looked perfectly normal from the outside but was filled mostly with chlorinated water mixed with a foul-smelling substance to discourage consumption, along with a small dry compartment so the money or prize would pop up when the consumer opened the can.

Not long after the MagiCans were released, an eleven-year-old boy from Massachusetts[2] got a can with a leak. As a result, his Coke tasted funny. His parents alerted state health officials, and Coca-Cola was forced to run newspaper and TV ads warning people that some

---

2   Anthony Ramirez, "Problems Pop Up in Coke Promotion," *The New York Times*, accessed November 30, 2019, http://www.nytimes.com/1990/05/24/business/problems-pop-up-in-coke-promotion.html.

of their cans might contain a harmless but foul-smelling liquid that shouldn't be consumed.

Coca-Cola spent several weeks pulling product off the shelves. During that time, my job as a highly paid engineer at the Coca-Cola Company was to drill holes in the bottoms of the MagiCans and put them on a rack so all the liquid could drain out of them. Once the cans were done draining, the next engineer's job was to turn the cans upside down and fill them with hot wax. The third engineer's job was to put a sticker on the bottom of those cans and randomly place them in twelve-packs. I can't imagine how expensive it was to pull all the products off the shelves and pay engineers not to do their day jobs but instead to drain cans and put stickers on them and then ship the cans out again.

Shortly after the MagiCan issue, some of my colleagues and I attended a project management course at Young, Clark & Associates (YCA), which is now Project Success, Inc. It was at this course that we learned the Project Success Method. We began to use these techniques on our projects and reap the benefits. In 1994 I joined the YCA/PSI team and began the journey that I'm still on, the one that forms the basis for this book.

The MagiCan promotion ended up being an embarrassment to Coca-Cola and everyone who worked on the project, but Coca-Cola is by no means the only example. In fact, a 2015 report showed that, out of fifty thousand projects, 71 percent failed to meet these three criteria: on time, on budget, and with satisfactory results.[3] This is one indication that most organizations don't understand how to effectively manage projects. With a failure rate that high, it is clear that a majority

---

3    Shane Hastie and Stephane Wojewoda, "Standish Group 2015 Chaos Report – Q&A with Jennifer Lynch," Info!, October 4, 2015, https://www.infoq.com/articles/standish-chaos-2015/.

of projects are being launched with poor project management or none at all. In my experience, gained from almost thirty years of helping organizations manage projects successfully, these six common issues account for many project failures:

1. Project managers don't "own" the people and resources needed to work on their projects.

2. Project management is viewed as punitive.

3. Project team members have changing priorities.

4. Project team members overestimate their availability and underestimate the amount of work needed to complete the project.

5. Project teams refuse to recognize that some projects need to be killed—and killed early.

6. Project managers don't "shift the worry curve."

Other common issues include lack of clarity, strong desire to do "real work" rather than wasting time planning, overlaunching with inadequate support, and a throw-it-over-the-fence mentality. We'll discuss all of these in this book, but for now I'd like to focus on the six listed here.

# 1. PROJECT MANAGERS DON'T "OWN" THE PEOPLE AND RESOURCES NEEDED TO WORK ON THEIR PROJECTS

Has this ever happened to you? You're leaving the office for a few days, and there's a list of tasks that need to be done. You send an email to a few people saying, "By next Friday this needs to get done. Can y'all please make sure that happens?" Of course, by the time next Friday rolls around, and you get back to the office, nothing's been done. The punch line here is everybody was asked to do it, anybody could have done it, somebody should have done it, but nobody actually did it.

What happened? Because none of the people on the email list *committed* to doing the tasks you asked for, they all assumed someone else would do them. This is particularly challenging when project managers don't "own" their resources—they don't have the ability to fire, hire, or reprimand their team members for failing to complete a task. The Project Success Method avoids this by getting every team member to verbally commit to certain activities before the project begins.

As I mentioned before, when we start our process, the first thing we do is charter the project to ensure alignment among the team on the scope and objectives. Once the charter has been approved by the customer(s), we define a work breakdown structure. With that structure, we identify every activity that must be done for the project to be completed. This is accomplished by starting with the really big buckets of work (e.g., deliverables) then further breaking them into more and more manageable chunks (e.g., subdeliverables). We continue this process until we have identified all the activities or tasks for the project (at least our best guess at that time).

# CENTURY MANUFACTURING COMPANY
## (Work Breakdown Structure)

### MELBOURNE PLANT DEVELOPMENT
### (Anders)

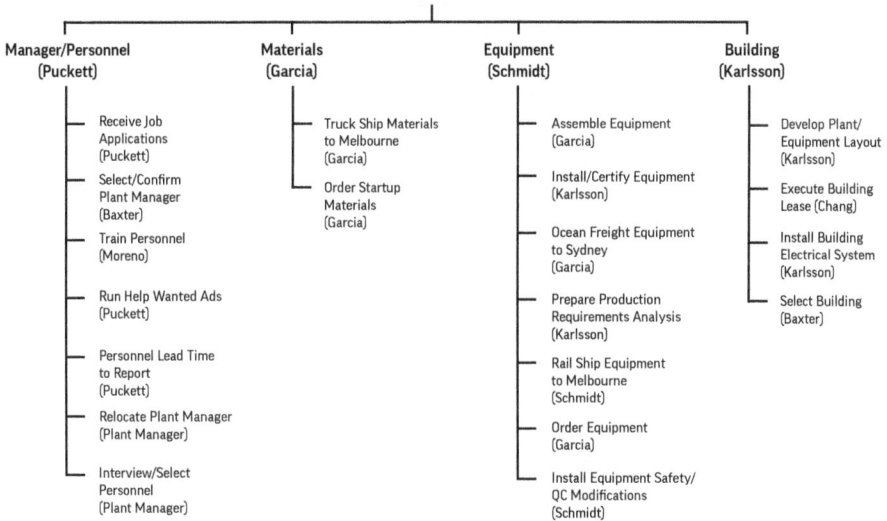

| Manager/Personnel (Puckett) | Materials (Garcia) | Equipment (Schmidt) | Building (Karlsson) |
|---|---|---|---|
| Receive Job Applications (Puckett) | Truck Ship Materials to Melbourne (Garcia) | Assemble Equipment (Garcia) | Develop Plant/ Equipment Layout (Karlsson) |
| Select/Confirm Plant Manager (Baxter) | Order Startup Materials (Garcia) | Install/Certify Equipment (Karlsson) | Execute Building Lease (Chang) |
| Train Personnel (Moreno) | | Ocean Freight Equipment to Sydney (Garcia) | Install Building Electrical System (Karlsson) |
| Run Help Wanted Ads (Puckett) | | Prepare Production Requirements Analysis (Karlsson) | Select Building (Baxter) |
| Personnel Lead Time to Report (Puckett) | | Rail Ship Equipment to Melbourne (Schmidt) | |
| Relocate Plant Manager (Plant Manager) | | Order Equipment (Garcia) | |
| Interview/Select Personnel (Plant Manager) | | Install Equipment Safety/ QC Modifications (Schmidt) | |

In the simple example above, there are only four deliverables, but a complex project can have many, many more. Under each deliverable is a list of the activities—in no particular order—that explains what needs to be done to complete the project. Eventually, each task will have an owner or an activity manager. The activity manager is the person that has agreed to take responsibility for the successful completion of an activity (or set of activities). They're the person who looks at the project manager and says, "That's my task. I own it. I'll make sure it gets done."

The challenge is that the person that has agreed to be responsible for successful delivery of the task doesn't technically work for the project manager. This happens because project management is usually conducted in a matrix environment where each team member officially reports (solid line on the organizational chart) to their functional manager for their annual reviews, pay raises, and the like but reports indirectly (dotted line on the org chart) to the project manager. In addition, each of those activity managers is also working on several other projects. So the project manager not only has no formal authority over the project team but is also competing for time with an activity manager's multiple other projects. When the project starts, a team member may tell you they'll have something completed by a certain date when in reality, they're balancing so many projects that they might not get around to it in the time frame originally promised. And if they don't get around to it, the project manager has no recourse against them for missing the deadline.

## 2. PROJECT MANAGEMENT IS VIEWED AS PUNITIVE

If you ask most people who have worked on a large project what they think about project management, they will say, "I hate it." One reason people don't like project management is that it's viewed as punitive. Because we work in a matrix, we're typically working on five or ten things at a time, so when a new project comes along, it's just one more thing to add to an already overwhelming workload.

In their experience, project management means that someone who is not their boss is going to assign them tasks and deadlines without their input, plug both into a computer to generate a Gantt Chart, and club them over the head with it for the remainder of the project. Because those activities are often planned without the team member's input, they end up being late on some tasks. Now, not only do they have the project manager yelling at them for being late, but that same project manager is also telling the team member's boss that the team member is not delivering.

When the project team members are working in an environment where they have little to no input yet are held accountable for results, is it any wonder they see project management as punitive?

Project management should be helpful, not punitive. Project managers should enable the people on the team to do their work successfully, and that comes down to paying attention to and managing the people side of things. If you involve the team early on in the process, ask members to be involved in the charter, let them identify their own tasks, and allow them to choose their own duration or time frame for completing an activity, it will give those team members the buy-in needed to be truly committed to your project.

# 3. PROJECT TEAM MEMBERS HAVE CHANGING PRIORITIES

Because everyone who works on a project is probably also working on five or more other projects, their priorities are constantly shifting. Whenever I lead a training session, I ask everyone in the room, "How many of you work in a multiproject environment, meaning you have more than one project that you're responsible for working on at a given time?"

Everyone raises a hand. Then I ask, "Of all the projects that are currently on your plate, how many are considered top priority?"

Everybody always laughs and either says, "All of them" or "Whoever was in my office last."

The problem is that *in a world where everything is top priority, nothing actually is.* This represents a huge challenge for project team members because if nothing is top priority, how do you decide which of the activities that are scheduled to be worked on this week will actually get done? After all, you have more on your plate in any given week than can possibly be accomplished.

Another challenge with changing priorities is that they're often driven by internal politics. Regardless of where "project A" is in terms of overall importance to the company, if "project A" is engineering or marketing driven, the functional managers of those teams are going to say they are the highest priority for the company because they want their departments to remain relevant. If a functional manager notices that the number of projects their team is responsible for is dwindling, it will become more and more important to them to make sure that each project is deemed a high priority. If their projects are consistently low priority, their perceived value to the organization is also low, so it's in their best interest to make every single project look like a high priority one even if it isn't.

Every company needs a third-party body inside the organization—a steering committee—that prioritizes projects and says, "Based on the potential profit (or whatever internal metric or value is determined) for the company, this is the first priority project. Put your best resources here. And, if we can only support five projects, these are the five we should do, in this priority order."

Unfortunately, many organizations take a shotgun approach to project management. They try to do everything in parallel, and nothing gets done well or on time. Or management continues to pile on projects, so they end up overlaunching and then deliver late because they lack the necessary resources to complete all the projects at the same time. This is how customers are lost.

# 4. PROJECT TEAM MEMBERS OVERESTIMATE THEIR AVAILABILITY AND UNDERESTIMATE THE AMOUNT OF WORK NEEDED TO COMPLETE THE PROJECT

When I started at PSI, I was thirty-one and at least ten to twenty years younger than my coworkers. To everyone at the company, I was just a kid. In fact, I was so low on the organization chart that they created a senior associate position so I'd be differentiated from the others. Everyone else was a consultant, senior consultant, or vice president. I was a senior associate for a year or two, and then I started working my way up and growing in the job. I went from senior associate to consultant to senior consultant to VP and then eventually bought the company.

The reason I was considered so green is that PSI hired and continues to hire people who have extensive postcollege, real-world project management experience as well as the technical expertise and people skills to manage multiple projects. This is unusual. Many project managers have one or two of these three skills. They may know about the technical aspects of any given project, but they can't manage people. Or they have project management experience, but the project they've been asked to manage is outside of their expertise, so they struggle to ask big-picture questions that are crucial to delivering a high-quality project on time and on budget. This disconnect happens because project managers are often selected based on their technical skills. The problem with this assumption is that many technical people want to stay on the technical side of things. When you become a project manager, your job is to manage the project to successfully deliver the gadget, not design the gadget. This is a hard shift for many technical people to accept, especially if they don't understand or enjoy the people side of project management.

I saw this firsthand at PSI. About ten years ago, I hired a guy named Vinny. He was a very good engineer with many years of technical design experience and had been a part of many projects in his career, so he fit the mold of people we liked to hire. After about a year, Vinny turned in his notice. When I asked him why he was leaving, he said, "I've come to the realization that I want to do the sticky note, not write the sticky note," meaning he wanted to go back to being an engineer doing the physical design. He did not want to be responsible for planning the overall project.

When we go through our process and get everyone in the room for that three-to-five-day initial planning meeting, we write hundreds or thousands of tasks on sticky notes and post them on the flip chart paper on the walls as we build our project plan. Each of those sticky notes is an activity that someone has to complete in order to get the project done. Project managers have neither the time nor the expertise to perform the tasks; they have to support the people doing them. Like many technical people, Vinny wanted to do the activities on the sticky note, not manage the team.

*Actual planning session results*
*Credit: David Halm*

Unfortunately, more often than not the project manager doesn't realize or want to admit their preference for doing a given activity—at least not initially. Instead over time they assign themselves more and more of the work that they like doing instead of ensuring the people on the team have what they need to be successful. This is detrimental for a project because it means no one is steering the ship.

## 5. PROJECT TEAMS REFUSE TO RECOGNIZE THAT SOME PROJECTS NEED TO BE KILLED—AND KILLED EARLY

Some projects, for whatever reason, shouldn't go through to completion, but no one wants their project killed. Why? Because if your project gets killed, you don't have any work to do. And what happens if your department doesn't have any work to do? You don't have a job.

Another reason people don't like killing projects is that after a while they get attached to the work they've done. After working on something for nine months, it becomes your baby; you're invested. The last thing you want to hear is that it's being canceled. Yet in some industries, if you're not the first to market, your company doesn't get *any* of the revenue. The first to market gets 100 percent of the revenue. Everybody else gets nothing. If the competition has already gone to market with its competing product, it's smart to kill a project even if it only has two or three months left. But no one wants to kill a project they've invested months of blood, sweat, and tears in.

Often, someone will argue that even though the customer is gone, nine months of resources have gone into the project, so the team should finish it just in case they need the intellectual property down the road. Then the question becomes "Should we really throw three additional months of good effort behind nine months of wasted effort?" Somebody has to make that hard decision. In my experience that project needs to be killed. The thirty to forty people who have been working on that project need to be reallocated to other projects that are going to make the company money because this project no longer will. However, project managers are often reluctant to kill projects because they have an investment in them; they don't want them to go away. The project manager and the team have pride of ownership over the project.

## 6. PROJECT MANAGERS DON'T "SHIFT THE WORRY CURVE™"

Let's say I ask one of my team members, Pat, if he can get X, Y, and Z done for me by this time next year. He says sure and thinks, "I have a year to do it. That's plenty of time."

We create human life in only nine months, so getting a few tasks done for one project in a year is no problem, right? Pat's a smart person; he knows what he's doing and thinks he can do anything in a year. And he's right—if that one thing were the only thing he had to do. But like the rest of us, Pat lives in a multiproject world. He never has just one thing to focus on.

It is likely that Pat is also in the middle of five other projects, and he's juggling dozens of things at a time. Some of Pat's other projects are just starting, some are in the middle, and some are almost finished. When Pat leaves the project kickoff meeting for this sixth project, he knows the project is super important because that's what the project manager told him, but the meeting lasted only twenty minutes, so it was short on details. Pat leaves the meeting with a sixth project that he knows almost nothing about. He hasn't been assigned any tasks, he doesn't know what all the activities are or how they fit together, and he hasn't been given any near-term deadlines. All Pat knows is that he's on the project team and the team has a year to complete the project. Of course, Pat is much more worried about the here and now, the ten things he has to do today for the five other projects he's working on, than he is about any one thing that involves this new project. So what happens? He puts off project number six because he reassures himself that he's got plenty of time.

If there were a tangible way to measure Pat's attention level about project number six when he leaves the kickoff meeting, the reading would be very low. It's too far in the future; plus, he hasn't been assigned any tasks—the project is currently a gray, nebulous "thing" that needs to be done sometime in the next twelve months. We call this the uninformed optimism phase.

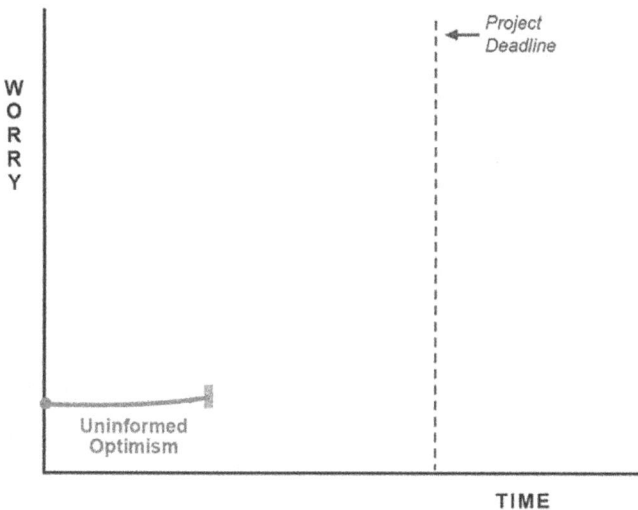

Before he knows it, six months have passed, and Pat realizes he's halfway through the project duration. All of that time has passed, and he hasn't done an appreciable amount of work. He's starting to wonder if he can get everything done on time. This is the phase of the project where Pat will avoid other team members or hope that if they're having a casual conversation, no one will bring up the project, and if they do bring it up, he's secretly hoping that they haven't worked on it either. This phase of the worry curve is called vague concern. We call it that because there's nothing that proves Pat will absolutely be late. He's still got six months to go, but his Spidey sense is tingling, indicating things aren't looking good, but there's no plan to compare against to confirm his suspicion.

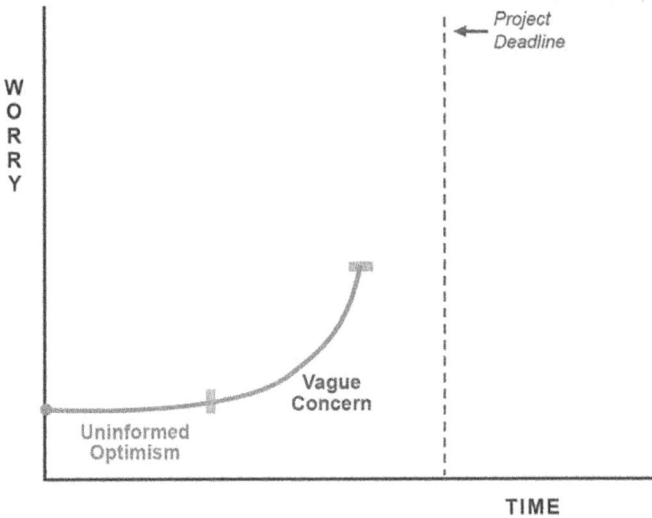

Now let's say the project deadline is six weeks out. When Pat realizes this, his worry level shoots through the roof. This phase of the worry curve is appropriately named the panic phase. It is the most expensive phase of the project both financially and emotionally. You do things during the panic phase that you would have never imagined doing at the beginning of the project. Your attitude almost becomes "I don't care what it costs, just get it done." I've seen projects where the company had to air-freight concrete block to a construction site and rent a dedicated C-130 aircraft to transport some equipment from the United States to Russia in order to hit the respective deadlines.

It's also expensive emotionally because this is the phase of the project when you lose talented team members, or their reputations get damaged. During the panic phase of the project, team members begin to cut corners because things are late, and they are feeling the pressure. Their attitude becomes "This is good enough. I don't have time to make it right. This will have to do." To make matters worse, in the panic phase, team members are working sixty to eighty hours a week. They think to themselves, "I'm killing myself to get this done but I can't even take pride in my work product," so they leave the company in search of a place where they can be both productive and proud of their work.

So how are reputations damaged during the panic phase? Let's say your activities are the last ones that must be completed before the project is done. Through no fault of your own, the things you need in order to complete your tasks are delivered six weeks late. You work nights and weekends to make up half of the delay, but the project is still three weeks late. Are you lauded for making up three weeks of lateness or only remembered for being three weeks late? Unfortunately, we both know the answer is that you are remembered for being late and not for your herculean efforts to make up the delay you received. I know that for some of you this is really resonating.

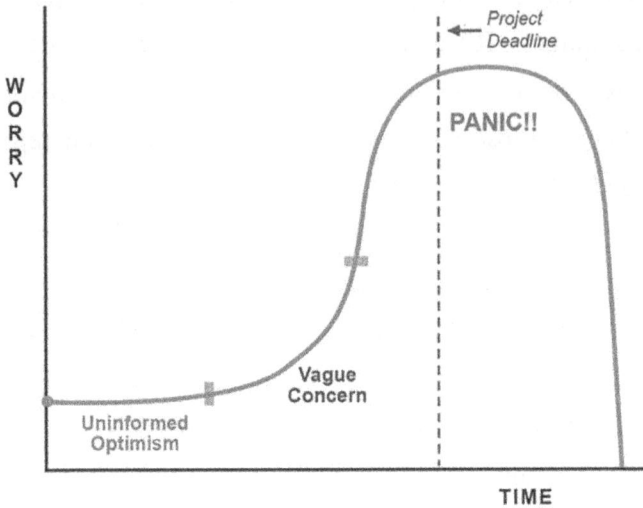

To avoid the panic phase, we need to shift the worry curve to the left; that is, we need to worry earlier. Instead of holding a twenty-minute kickoff meeting, we bring everyone together for two or three days to plan the project. Individual team members commit to specific, well-defined responsibilities and a detailed schedule. The team also commits to meeting regularly (say, every two weeks) throughout the project to report the status of current activities, to determine the status of the project, to solve problems as they arise, and to update the project plan.

The planning process itself raises the worry level, as the team analyzes the requirements, constraints, assumptions, and risks associated with the project. As a result, team members understand the challenges they face. Team members also feel more pressure for progress from the very beginning of the project because they know the team will meet, and they will have to report on their progress in just two weeks—and every two weeks after that.

Often, a project team member will have a deliverable due soon after the project begins. The task could be to select a supplier, complete the first iteration of design, develop business requirements, write design specifications, and so on. The team member's worry level rises as the deadline approaches. When they complete the deliverable, the worry level drops back down—at least until their next deliverable comes due, and the process repeats. Team members travel along the peaks and valleys of worry throughout the project as their activities come due and are completed. Sometimes the team member's worry level will rise to the panic level. For example: the customer may change the project requirements; the team may lose a key member; an unexpected technical issue may surface. Once the issue has been resolved, the level of worry will decrease back to normal

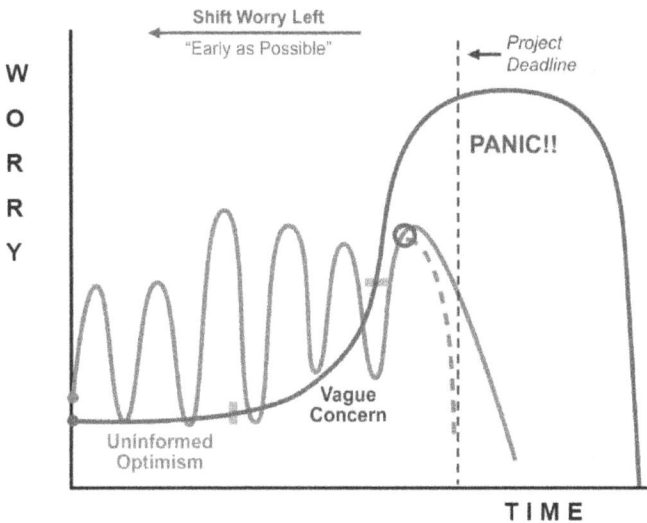

The best way to shift the worry curve is for someone in senior management to say, "Enough is enough. Let's take the time to plan the project correctly by investing the time on the front end. We'll see the benefits on the back end in earlier delivery, higher quality, and/or lower cost." Unfortunately, many project managers can't convince their team to shift the worry curve because they either don't know how to manage people, are unable to work within a matrix organization, or don't understand the concept themselves.

---

"You must be single minded.
Drive for the one thing on
which you have decided."

—General George S. Patton

---

## HOW I FIRST LEARNED THE IMPORTANCE OF SHIFTING THE WORRY CURVE

When I began my career at PSI, I was on the Coca-Cola Olympics planning team for the 1996 Olympic Games in Atlanta. Back then, we did our planning in what we called the war room, a converted conference room with beautiful cherry wood paneling. We didn't have sticky notes or sticky paper back then, so when we were ready to start planning, we cut off big lengths of butcher paper and taped them on the walls of this beautiful conference room. Then we sprayed adhesive onto the butcher paper and stuck up white sheets of flip chart paper. We then created a hand-drawn diagram for the network of activities in collaboration with the team.

The Monday before one of our planning sessions for the Olympics, my boss said, "Hey, Clint, on Friday we have a big planning session scheduled. Make sure the war room is set up before the session." I had other things on my plate since that meeting wasn't the only thing I was working on that week. I thought I had plenty of time and waited until Thursday to start setting up the war room. However, when I tried to get into the room at around noon, it was locked. Everyone was at an off-site meeting that I wasn't aware of, so there was nobody to let me into the room. Of course, I panicked. I stayed until seven in the evening in the hopes that someone would return to the office. When no one did, I made sure I was the first one to arrive the next morning. Unfortunately, my boss was the second. When he asked if the room was ready, I told him what had happened. He said, "Well, I have a key; you could have asked me to let you in," but he wasn't around when I was trying to get in.

So my boss let me into the room, and we got it ready for the meeting. I thought I was off the hook because he didn't say anything else about it. About a week later, he turned to me in our shared office and said, "Clint, remember last week when the conference room wasn't ready?" to which I nodded yes. He continued, "We teach earliest possible start—you need to live it."

From that point on, the whole philosophy of shifting the worry curve really clicked for me. If you can do it today, do it today, and get it out of the way in case unforeseen issues arise.

# CHAPTER 2 KEY TAKEAWAYS

- Projects fail for six reasons:

  1. Project managers don't "own" the people and other resources needed to work on their project.

  2. Project teams differ from operational teams.

  3. Project team members have competing/changing priorities.

  4. Project team members overestimate their availability while underestimating the amount of work needed to complete the project.

  5. Project teams are reluctant to recognize that some projects need to be killed.

  6. Project managers don't "shift the worry curve.

- Most people view project management as a punitive experience.

- In today's project environment, every project team member is working on multiple activities for a variety of other projects.

- When everything is top priority, nothing is.

- Project managers often don't have both the technical skills and people skills necessary to effectively manage projects.

"Success demands
singleness of purpose."

—VINCE LOMBARDI

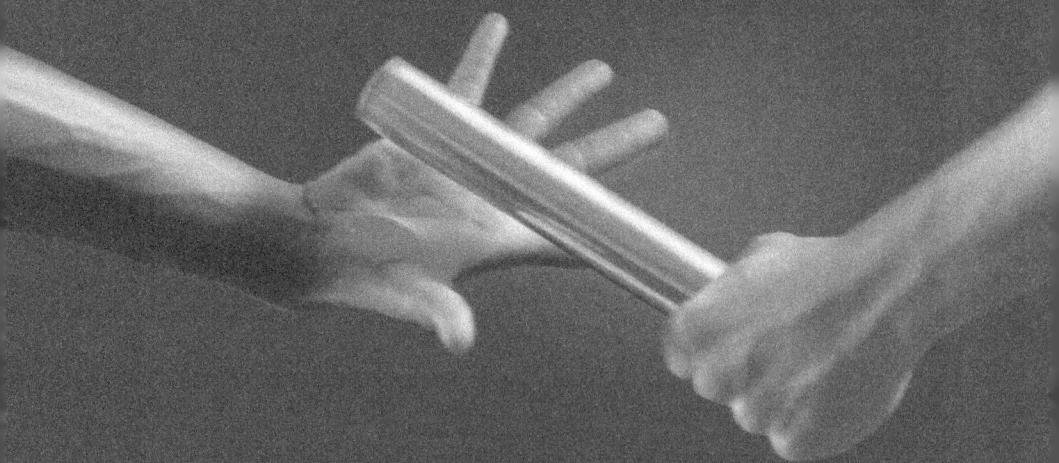

"Success is simple.
Do what's right, the right
way, at the right time."

—ARNOLD H. GLASOW

# CHAPTER 3:

# KNOW WHAT'S IN YOUR TOOL KIT

*LET'S STEP INTO* the world of project management according to the Project Success Method. Let's say BulldozR, Inc., fictitious designer and manufacturer of heavy machinery, decides it wants to increase its market share by 3 percent, from 14 percent to 17 percent. How will the company do it?

First, they send the sales and marketing teams out to poll BulldozR's customers and develop the voice of the customer. Finished with market research, these teams come back to BulldozR and say, "If we add these three features to the XGen product, we could sell another one hundred thousand units, and that would move our market share to 17 percent."

Typically, most, if not everyone, on the project team understands the Project Success Method. No matter where they're based, they all fly in for a three-day planning session. When they arrive, they have a working knowledge of the project from documents sent to them before they traveled, and the planning session opens with the project manager giving a brief overview of the project. For the next three to four hours, the team develops the project charter and documents the scope of the project (i.e., what needs to be done to increase market share by 3 percent). They also identify project objectives, key stakeholders, the desired deadline, compression savings rates, assumptions, concerns/risks, and constraints—basically all the things that need to be understood to complete the project successfully.

Since the (internal) customer is in the room and an active participant in the charter process, we have their commitment and buy-in; therefore, we assume the charter will be approved so we can immediately continue the process. Next, the work breakdown structure is developed by the cross-functional, knowledgeable team members. At this point, the engineers on the team start thinking about design activities, the marketing folks think about the marketing activities, the manufacturing engineers identify the tasks to ensure manufacturability, the HR team member documents the recruiting and training tasks, and so on. Each team member in the room thinks, "Now that I have a clear understanding of the project (thanks to their participation in the charter session), these are the things I need to make sure get done in order to complete the project." All these activities are compiled into the work breakdown structure—the list of activities that must be done to complete the project. The work breakdown structure won't be 100 percent complete—it includes everything everyone can think of in that moment—but it's a living, breathing document. Even in a perfect world, we know that something will be missed during the work breakdown session, but that's OK because it will be discovered and added during planning and control. We have to keep moving forward because perfect is the enemy of good enough, and if we wait for perfection, the project will never start.

Once the team members identify their activities, they move into the networking phase, where they spend another day or so putting the activities in the right order. The result of this step is a network diagram (a visual sequence of events) that includes a predecessor and successor for each task. There is an owner for each task (an activity manager), and each task has a duration. This network diagram gets put into the computer, and the team moves into validation. They realize that some of the dates don't make sense, or some of the activities appear to be out of sequence. As the team digs into the plan, they discover that some activities were connected improperly (perhaps a data entry error), an incorrect duration was entered, the wrong team member was assigned, and so on. Once each of these pieces is fixed, the team moves into compression, the final step. They apply the deadline they've been given to increase market share by 3 percent and compress the project schedule to meet it. Say the deadline for this project is July 1, but the computer says the project won't finish until October 22 based on the way that it is currently planned. Instead of the project manager deciding how to remove the lateness, the

**They are committed to and believe in the plan *because they built it!***

entire team sits down and hashes out how to compress the schedule. Individual team members commit to doing things differently in order to get the project back on track. Eventually, the team compresses the schedule back far enough to meet the deadline, and the team begins execution of *their* actionable plan. They are committed to and believe in the plan *because they built it*!

Hopefully, you can see how attractive this approach is to the project team members and how it leads to a deeper level of commitment on their part. But there are still a couple of things I would change if I could. What would need to change to make it completely perfect? In our example, the deadline and budget were given to us, but in the perfect world, the schedule built by the team determines the project deadline and budget.

Believe it or not, that was the easy part. Now comes the really difficult piece—managing the project and dealing with the bad news that inevitably comes your way during project execution. Over the life of the project, things are constantly changing, and that impacts your plan. Team members get sick, they get jury duty, they get pulled off the project to put out a customer fire, or they run into unexpected design and approval issues. In addition, vendors deliver late, a problem is more difficult to solve than anticipated, and you realize you're missing some activities in your plan. Each of these can negatively impact your budget and timeline (assuming your specs are nonnegotiable). Consequently, project control is a constant dance that requires a diverse set of management tools.

## USE YOUR LEVERS WISELY

A couple of years ago, PSI worked on a Caterpillar project that was located in Wamego, Kansas. I don't know how Wamego laid claim to *The Wizard of Oz*—the author isn't from there and didn't live there—but they have. In front of one local eatery, Toto's TacOZ!, the sidewalk is painted yellow, as in the yellow brick road. It's located two doors down from the Oz Museum and a block away from the Oz Winery. On one corner, they even have a full-size replica of the house that landed on the Wicked Witch of the East, complete with her ruby-slipper-clad feet sticking out from underneath. Although Wamego didn't appear to have a wizard, working among *The Wizard of Oz* memorabilia got me thinking about traditional project management, and how some project managers are like the Wizard of Oz. They project an image of competence and all-knowingness while hidden behind the curtain of mystery. Meanwhile, the project team is quivering in fear and uncertainty.

In *The Wizard of Oz*, the wizard sits behind the curtain pulling levers. He never leaves his place behind the curtain. He never actually talks to anyone. He gathers his information unseen and then uses his levers, visual effects, and loud noises to put on a really impressive show to convince others of how great he is. Unfortunately, some project managers operate in the same manner as the Wizard of Oz. Those observing the display put on by the project manager are impressed by the colorful graphs, charts, and other data. We can't help but fall in love with the project dashboard and its green, yellow, and red lights.

As project managers, we do indeed have levers to pull on our projects, but they're not called authority, fear, and intimidation. They are time, cost, and quality. These levers are interconnected, so if one is pulled, it affects the other two. For example, if you decide to spend $150,000 to air-freight equipment for a project, the cost lever will go up, but the time lever will go down. The quality lever will stay the same.

It's impossible for a project manager to effectively move these levers if he or she never steps out from behind the curtain. If the manager is not talking to team members and understanding how and why certain activities need to change, it doesn't matter how they move the levers. The project as delivered will not be on time, on budget, and of high quality.

## THE THREE-HOUR HOUSE

Whenever I teach the lever concept, I ask my class, "What do you think the world record is for time spent building a house? How fast do you think it can be done?"

Then I give the specs of a real-world example in order to answer that question. The house is a fifteen-hundred-square-foot ranch with siding (instead of brick). It's got three bedrooms, two baths, and a two-car garage. It's also fully landscaped. Build time starts the minute the construction team steps foot on the property. The only thing that's been done before the team arrives is that the foundation has been staked, but it hasn't been poured, and the materials have been staged on-site. The team has to build everything from the materials (no prefab). Assume the project has unlimited resources and instantaneous permits, a luxury no project ever really has. So how long does it take to lay the foundation, build the walls and the roof, install the plumbing and the electricity, put the drywall up, paint the house inside and out, and get it move-in ready?

I always get a wide variety of answers, anything from three days to three months and everything in between. Then I say, "You're not even using the right units. The units are actually hours."

In 1983, in an effort to promote the construction industry, the San Diego Board of Trade held a contest to attempt to break the then world record of building a house in four hours and eighteen minutes. Seven-hundred workers split between two teams descended on two vacant lots in Paradise Valley to see who could build the house the quickest. The winning team did it in two hours, fifty-two minutes, and thirty-one seconds.[4] Building a house at this speed pulls the time lever *way* down, but what happens to cost and quality? Well, hiring seven-hundred people to work on two houses for several hours certainly isn't cheap. Not

---

4    Jeffrey Miller, "Speed-Built Homes Flawed, Owners Claim," Nov. 29, 1986, accessed Dec. 2, 2019, https://www.latimes.com/archives/la-xpm-1986-11-29-me-16253-story.html.

to mention hiring multiple cement trucks, employing fast-cure concrete, and the fact they built two houses for practice. Plus the cost of the project managers and their staff in preparing for the events. While I'm not sure what it cost to build the houses, I do know that what the teams made up for in time, they lost in quality.

By May 1984 the owners of the homes were already having problems. One owner, Angie van Gaasback, said that the first night she and her husband stayed in the house, the hot water pipes burst, causing flooding in one bathroom. She also said the house had buckled walls, a flawed roof, mismatched paint, a faulty sewer, and a flooded backyard.

So, while the van Gaasbacks had a home in less than three hours, quality suffered severely. While the rest of us may have to wait a year to move into a new home, if the time, quality, and cost levers are more balanced, we might not wake up to a flooded bathroom the first night we spend in our new house.

---

## TECHNOLOGY: A TOOL, NOT THE BE-ALL AND END-ALL

Quick, what's the most commonly used software for project management? The answer is Microsoft Excel. Excel isn't actually a project management tool. It's a tool that people *use* for project management. Software tools developed specifically for managing projects with much more functionality, like Microsoft Project or Primavera P6, will make your life easier.

A common mistake in project management is to hire someone fresh out of college, give them a copy of Microsoft Project, and say, "Go forth and be a project manager." Because this person lacks the knowledge base and training needed to be a good project manager, they are forced to rely on technology. I know from experience that software is most assuredly not the answer to successful project management. Software is good at automating a process, but it cannot account for the people and variables that move that process along.

> A common mistake in project management is to hire someone fresh out of college, give them a copy of Microsoft Project, and say, "Go forth and be a project manager."

The software tools available today are great at math. They calculate complex plans with the push of a button or click of the mouse, but the answer is only as good as the data it's based on. If the person entering the numbers didn't get the right durations for the project activities with accurate predecessors and successors based on what the team believed to be true, the output will be invalid.

## AGILE VERSUS WATERFALL

There are two main approaches to project management: Agile and Waterfall. An Agile lover would describe Waterfall as a more traditional (a.k.a. old school or dated) approach to project management. It requires that the entire project be planned in great detail on day one. Once planned, there are no modifications to the plan, and no feedback is solicited. There are no conversations about it. People do their work according to the plan without any feedback loops, course corrections, or changes based on what is learned throughout the process. With Waterfall, they say, you put in the numbers for a project that's due in two years and assume that nothing will change in those two years. People will meet every deadline, there won't be any hiccups, and everything will go exactly as planned. What usually happens with Waterfall, according to the Agile fan, is that the customer is unhappy with the final product because they are forced to live with what was delivered even if it isn't what they wanted. What I've just described isn't truly Waterfall, just what someone that subscribes to Agile would have you believe. I have never seen a project planned and executed this way.

> "We are kept from our goal, not by obstacles but by a clear path to a lesser goal."
>
> —Robert Brault

Agile, on the other hand, places all activities, called features, into a backlog and then the team decides, based on customer input, which features are most important. These features are pulled off the backlog and put into a sprint, a window of time in which something needs to get done. Usually, sprints are two to four weeks long, but they are always the same length throughout the project (either all of them are two weeks or all are four weeks). At the end of each sprint, if those features are not complete, they go back into the backlog list, and the newest top priority leads the next sprint. While Agile has the team working on the features most important to the customer, it's not a project management methodology. No one using Agile can tell me when the project will actually be done because project scope isn't fully understood early in the project, and the product backlog is never really finalized. As a result, no one really tries to determine the exact number of sprints required, and there is certainly no commitment to the project being complete at a certain time. Furthermore, no one is proactively adding additional sprints to resolve the items that were added back into the backlog at the end of each completed sprint. Items are simply moved from the backlog to the next sprint until all items are completed, or the customer says stop.

## AGILE BEFORE AGILE

PSI's process was Agile long before there was an Agile methodology. We've been successfully managing projects since 1983, and we have always recommended that project managers not plan in great detail for something that's two years in the future because things always change. Instead, we advocate planning in detail the things you know the most about; that is, the things that are already in process or about to start. However, activities that are in the distant future, and therefore currently unclear or nebulous, are captured as longer duration or high-level activities. If you put a bunch of detail into something that's eighteen months in the future, you'll have to go back and rework it multiple times because it's largely guesswork that rarely turns out right. With our process, we expect that at some point what was once eighteen months in the future and unclear will become very clear when it's only two months away. You can take that high-level activity and break it up into more detail once you have the requisite knowledge, and you can do it without wasting your time.

Like Agile, we also recommend and always have recommended that near-term activities be somewhere between five and ten working days (which happens to be the same length as a typical sprint). You don't want a bunch of one-day tasks, because that's micromanaging—

it's tedious to plan this way and keep the schedule updated. You don't want a bunch of twenty-to-thirty-day tasks either because it's too easy for someone to procrastinate. Just as we discussed the importance and power of shifting the worry curve on a project, you want to shift the worry curve at the activity level. During the control meetings, which we recommend happen every one to two weeks, we update the plan to reflect what's actually happened, what we've learned that needs to be added to the plan, and where we need more time. In other words, we make the plan accurate and up to date, which Agile doesn't do. Instead, Agile gives you the sprints and a backlog. The idea with Agile is that if something isn't completed by the end of its assigned sprint, it's added back into the backlog. The backlog is then reprioritized, and items are selected for the next sprint. The issue with this process, as I've mentioned before, is that there's no telling how long the project will take. To know that, you would need to plan all your sprints. You would have to create a plan of what from the backlog goes into which sprint and then how many extra sprints have to be added to compensate for the activities that weren't finished during sprint L, M, and N.

While Agile is a good system for developing software and allowing the customer to receive a working piece of code (for a certain feature, for example) that they can test and give instantaneous feedback on, it's *not* project management. As a customer who has had software developed for our company, I find this to be quite comforting, knowing that each feature was either performing as expected or immediate creative action would be taken. Agile in software development is great, but when people try to apply it in bigger, broader ways, it breaks down. For example, a few years ago I was talking with one of my clients, and he was telling me about a kiosk project he was working on at his casino in Las Vegas. The kiosk was supposed to go on the casino floor, and he needed hardware, software, and the physical kiosk itself to be developed. In addition to building those three main components, the project team had to secure permits, run electricity to the kiosk locations, and procure several other pieces of the project such as signage. They had dozens of moving parts to contend with; however, the only thing they could really use Agile for was the software development part of the kiosk. After all, how do you fit a permit that may take months to obtain, or the physical kiosk build itself, into a ten-day sprint? It doesn't make any sense.

## THE LEAST OFFENSIVE WATERFALL GUY

Since 2012 I have been fortunate to serve as an adjunct professor in the executive education program at Georgia Tech. In this role I'm asked to speak to various programs about project management. During one of these sessions, a woman mentioned Agile and asked what I thought about it. But first, she painted a story that Waterfall was static, that it forced everyone to plan every activity to the nth degree—nothing ever gets changed, you don't revisit it for two years, and when you do, it doesn't match what you wanted.

I explained how PSI was Agile before Agile. Then I told her I'd never seen any project work that wasn't revisited for two years. The Project Success Method recommends that near-term activities should only be between five and ten days long. It also has everyone coming back together every two weeks to update the project and correct activities, so the plan is more accurate.

At the end of the session, this woman said, "Well, Clint, I have to tell you—you are the least offensive Waterfall guy I've ever met." I wear that like a badge of honor for people who love Agile.

---

## SCRUM IS NOT THE MASTER

I can't talk about Agile without mentioning Scrum. While I agree with many of the tenets of Agile (after all, we've been preaching them since before Agile was born), I do have some concerns about Scrum because it makes assumptions that don't really work. In "The Scrum Manifesto"—anything that claims to be a manifesto gives me pause—there is no project manager. There's a Scrum master who is responsible for making sure the team follows the Scrum process, but following a process isn't project management.

With Scrum, no one person has ownership of the whole project. Instead, fully self-directed teams that only work on one project at a time do the work. So they are fully dedicated and self-directed. Based on my experience, these are both problematic. At most companies, resources are tight, so having a resource fully dedicated to a single project is rare, but having multiple resources dedicated just doesn't happen. Furthermore, history tells me that if no one is in charge of a group, inevitably someone takes control and becomes the de facto leader. I'd prefer that person be the named project manager with the requisite authority needed to navigate the project to completion.

My experience is that, most of the time, if you leave people to their own devices, they will not finish all of their assigned tasks as scheduled. It's not that they're lazy; it's that they work in a multiproject environment where they have fifteen things to do today, and human nature says they're going to start with the easiest one or the one they enjoy the most or the one their boss is yelling about. The other tasks, particularly the hard ones or the ones that take the longest, will likely be put off.

Scrum doesn't work well because even though it empowers people it doesn't account for human nature. Someone needs to oversee the project to ensure that the right activities are being completed at the right time, which also means we need to know the critical path of the project.

## WHY PEOPLE ARE YOUR GREATEST TOOL

PSI uses a blended Agile-like Waterfall process that both leverages and supports the greatest asset in your tool kit—your people. People are the greatest tool in your tool kit because they know what they need from others to get their work done and how long it will take them to finish each task. They are the only ones who can accurately provide the data needed to predict activity completion with any accuracy. Only they have a complete understanding of what's currently on their plate, how many other projects they are committed to, or when they can't stay late due to personal or family commitments. They are also the only ones you can hold accountable for their activities. How long does each task take? Only the people performing it know.

For example, let's say I'm working on a project, and after entering the network diagram we discussed previously into Microsoft Project, I assign the resources needed to complete each task. I know that task 1 will require six hours of Sarah's time and eight hours of Andy's time, task 2 will take Joanna three hours and Chris four hours, task 3 will take Brett eleven hours, and task 4 will take Amy seventeen hours. I do this for every single activity, so that when I finish entering the tasks,

Microsoft Project adds the hours each resource needs to dedicate to the overall project each week to get the project done. The result for Sarah is that she needs to work sixty-three hours the first week to complete all of her assigned work. Clearly, we're already in trouble when it comes to Sarah, but to truly understand the situation, I need to know Sarah's availability, which is likely going to be somewhere south of 100 percent.

When I talk to Sarah (something a machine cannot do), I learn she will only be available 50 percent for this project because she is also working on three other projects. This means that for week one, the difference between the sixty-three hours we need from Sarah and the twenty hours she can give us is forty-three hours. Microsoft Project will highlight this overload and show that to get her assigned work done for week one, we'll essentially need three Sarahs at her current availability because even putting her on it 100 percent of the time won't fix the problem.

What I have just described is resource planning.[5] Software can be a powerful tool for resource management, but it only works if the data or the plan you've given it is good. If your plan is junk, the start and finish dates for the activities won't be correct, and the sixty-three hours calculated for Sarah in week one won't be correct either. Resource planning is nice to have and can be helpful, but it's the icing on the cake. First, you've got to develop a good plan, which should be done in a collaborative way by working with the team members and letting the software help with the math.

---

5    Resource planning is very time-consuming and tedious. We've found
     an easier solution is to implement the role of an activity manager. The
     activity manager gives a duration for each task based on the resources
     they have at their disposal. This approach is much less labor-intensive
     and follows the Pareto Principle—80 percent of the result for 20 percent
     of the effort.

## PEOPLE OFFER SOLUTIONS

Developing a good plan comes from talking to the people on the project and understanding how much time each activity will *realistically* take them. Software cannot go to Sarah and say, "Sarah, right now I've got you for twenty hours on this project this week. This is a really important point in the project; is there any way you can give me more time this week?" Software cannot develop a relationship with Sarah that might compel her to try really hard to give me a few more hours. Software also doesn't know that Sarah has a vendor or outside resources that can help her with one of the activities, removing six hours of time from the forty-three-hour overage. Software doesn't know that even though Sarah wants to help, she can't because she has an off-site training event this week, so she'll be away from her desk three of the five working days. Software can highlight an overload, but it cannot tell you how to solve it. Only a person can do that. And that person is the one who has agreed to take ownership of the tasks—the activity manager.

## ONLY PEOPLE CAN TELL YOU WHAT'S CHANGED

When you plan a project, even if you plan it well using the Project Success Method, it will only be accurate for about twenty-four hours. Then something will happen. Someone will get sick, someone will get pulled off for another project, or you will realize that you're missing some activities or that some of the durations that were given weren't right to begin with. Something will always need to change, so rather than leave the plan static in whatever software tool you've chosen, you'll need to return to your team periodically (typically weekly or every other week) and modify the plan so that it's correct again. And by that I mean that you put in the actuals (how long the task actually took, when it actually started and finished) and make course corrections. You may spend only three or four days planning the project, but you'll spend the next eighteen months executing it, so you have to go back periodically and update the plan to reflect your new knowledge of the project.

For this example, say the plan was for Sarah to start her task on Monday and finish on Friday. When I talk to Sarah, I learn that she did indeed start her activity on Monday, as scheduled, but something came up on another project that she had to deal with, so she couldn't finish it until the following Tuesday. Consequently, her activity was two days late. So I put that delay in the plan. Or maybe I talk to Sarah, and she tells me that she found out about a new two-day task that has to be done in order for her to complete her initial task. Well, the new task isn't in the project plan. It has to be added. Unfortunately, that task ends up on the critical path, so the project completion is delayed by two days. Now the project manager has to find a way to make up for that schedule slippage. Without Sarah's input, the project manager doesn't know that the project is off track.

## Software is not project management.

Software lets you quickly see the results of the course corrections to your plan, which is a valuable tool in project management, but these corrections are only as accurate as the information you input, which is most accurate when it comes directly from your team.

I've had numerous people tell me that they've stopped using Microsoft Project because when they make one change a lot of other dates change on other activities. That's what is supposed to happen! Project plans aren't static. You want to be able to make a single change and see the resulting impact on the affected activities. If you cannot, you may as well go back to building task lists in Excel. You have to build your plan using a sound, proven process with data provided in a collaborative way by the team members themselves. Project management software is a supporting tool that automates the calculations and should be used as such.

Software is not project management. Software is a tool that can help good project managers—*who understand people* and build plans in a collaborative way—ensure that their projects will be delivered on time, on budget, and with the highest quality.

## PEOPLE AREN'T PERCENTAGES

One of my favorite people in project management is Teresa Lynch. I've had the pleasure of working with her for almost twenty years at YUM Brands, Sony Pictures, and now Comcast. She understands project management like few I've encountered, and she does it right. There's no way Teresa would ever let any of her team members get away with telling her they're 50, 60, or 70 percent done with an activity.

This is what she tells them: "I could tell you that I'm 99 percent done with my PhD." She always pauses here to let that sink in. Then she says, "Now what I haven't told you is that I'm never going to be done, because I did my PhD work fifteen years ago and stopped. I'm never going to go back and complete it. So telling me you're 99 percent complete doesn't help me. I need to know when you're going to be done. That's the most important thing that I need to know."

I love that story because Teresa is exactly right. "Percent complete" is a worthless measurement. It is dangerous in the hands of an inexperienced team member and can be used to obfuscate in the hands of an experienced but less than honorable team member. It is really unfortunate that some project management software tools require the use of percent complete. I have two issues with using percent complete to update a project plan. First, it doesn't tell us when the task will actually be finished. But even more disturbing, it doesn't drive accountability, which is so important in a matrix environment. Remember, as project managers, we have neither the carrot nor the whip, so we're relying on the team member to hold themselves accountable.

Project managers who use our process never allow for anything to be reported as X percent complete. If I ask you for a status update on one of your tasks, you can answer me in several ways:

- I started it on November 15, and I'm going to finish it in three more days.

- I started it on November 15, and I'm going to finish it on November 20.

- I started it on November 15 and am 50 percent complete.

The first two responses give me a completion date; the third does not. You could be 50 percent complete for three more days or three more years. The first two responses give me a commitment. The third doesn't because percent complete never gives a commitment for completion. As the project manager, I can't go to the person who is waiting on you to finish this task and tell them when you'll be done so they know when they can start.

# CHAPTER 3 KEY TAKEAWAYS

- Projects are constantly changing, and each of these changes can affect scope, budget, and timeline.

- Agile is a great process for software development but is not a project management methodology.

- Time, cost, and quality are all interrelated; changing one typically affects the others. To deliver faster, cost normally increases or quality suffers.

- Software is not the solution to successful projects, people are.

- People can improve the way software processes durations and deadlines by offering solutions, providing good data for the software, and telling their project manager what has caused their activity completion and/or duration to change.

- Durations based on percentages are useless because they fail to provide the accurate data needed to predict when the task will actually be complete. They also do not provide accountability or commitment.

---

"[Electric communication] will never be a substitute for the face of a man, with his soul in it, encouraging another man to be brave and true."

—Charles Dickens

---

"In the midst of chaos, there
is also opportunity."

—SUN TSU

CHAPTER 4:

# GATHER THE RIGHT TEAM

*GEORGE IS AN ENGINEER* for a Fortune 500 food supplier. He has great technical skills and has a reputation for delivering innovative solutions. His boss is impressed by the work George has done and decides the next logical step in George's progression is to become a project manager, so he assigns him a project to manage. George is happy working in his engineering silo, but since he's been made project manager, he throws himself into the role. He knows the other people that have been assigned to work on the project with him are extremely busy. He also recalls how painful all of the team meetings and project management meetings were for him to attend as they distracted him from doing his "real job," the design work. He promises himself that he won't do the same thing to his team.

So George sits down in his silo and starts to plan the project. He creates a list of tasks and assigns predecessors and successors to those tasks all by himself. Then he looks at his list of team members and based on the skills he either knows them to have or is told they have he starts assigning tasks. With those tasks he includes how much time he thinks they'll need to complete each task. He assigns Jerry to do task X in two weeks and Crystal to do tasks A and B in four weeks.

Then he sends the schedule to his team, asking them to review it and let him know if they see any issues. When no feedback is forthcoming, George assumes all is well and congratulates himself for putting together such a good project plan while saving his team the tedium of all those planning sessions. In the days and weeks that follow, George greets his team members when he passes them in the hall; sometimes he asks how the project is going, but he never has truly meaningful conversations with them.

As the project moves along and George reaches his first set of deadlines, a feeling of unease sets in. He doesn't have a single email from any of his team members indicating that they've either finished their tasks or need more time to finish them. Since George hasn't bothered to have any serious discussions with his team to get their input on the project, the project has already fallen off track, and it's only just started!

So, what happened? What always happens in a silo—George made assumptions about his team's capabilities and availability and built the plan without their input; consequently, they had no buy-in to the project. They don't feel accountable for tasks that were assigned to them without their input. They certainly don't feel obligated to meet deadlines they feel are completely arbitrary. Instead of cooperation and collaboration, George gets nothing but silent resistance from his team.

One of the reasons the Project Success Method is so successful is that, at its core, it is team centric and establishes a commitment amongst the team members to a plan *they* develop. A key component of this success is to select a project manager that not only understands this principle but embraces it. There are two ways to select a project manager: hire from within the company or appoint someone from outside the organization to manage the project.

## SELECTING FROM WITHIN

Many companies select their project managers internally and then turn them loose to complete whatever project their company needs doing. One advantage of choosing a project manager internally is that person's tribal knowledge, which an outsider could never have. An internally selected project manager knows the company culture, the terminology, and what's happened with previous projects, in addition to having industry-specific knowledge.

We work with a Fortune 1000 company in Silicon Valley that designs, manufactures, and sells integrated circuits for numerous industries including healthcare and automotive. They almost always choose project managers from inside the company. The advantage to this approach is that the project manager understands the technical components of whatever project they are managing. For this particular company, this means project managers understand chip design. They know about software development, SOC (system on a chip), digital design, and analog design. They understand everything about making a chip because they live in that world. In that sense, this type of project manager has a head start over someone from outside of the organization. The downside to this approach is that because they have all this knowledge, they find it difficult not to drive things in a certain direction. If going in one direction has always worked for them personally, they have a tendency to push the team to do the same because it feels comfortable, even if going in that direction isn't necessarily the best decision for that particular project. A good project manager is unbiased, will support whichever direction is best for the team and the project, and not let their personal opinion unduly influence things.

## HIRING FROM OUTSIDE THE COMPANY

There are several advantages to this approach. First, there is obviously a much larger pool to draw from. The number of employees who currently work for the company does not limit you. You are able to choose from a more varied set of backgrounds along with a potentially broader range of knowledge and work experience.

One perceived drawback to hiring someone from outside the company as project manager is that outsiders don't know all the ins and outs of the processes needed to complete each task. Now, as long as the person managing the project can understand how everything fits together, I don't see this as a drawback. That being said, if the project manager has no technical experience at all, it might be problematic for the company.

Someone with a degree in finance or accounting, both of which are fine degrees, might have a really difficult time understanding a highly technical project like designing a governor system for an aircraft. In that situation, the outsider who has no technical knowledge at all will have to trust everything they've been told. Unfortunately, at the end of the day, this project manager won't know if one of the engineers is misleading them, which could impact the entire project.

A project manager without relevant project knowledge is at risk of becoming one who simply regurgitates data. They are ineffective because they cannot see the big picture. Even if they follow a process like ours, they can't effectively manage projects. They can't effectively lead the team because they can't understand how the activities fit together. It's not that they don't want to; they just simply can't.

I recall working with one individual on a project. He was intelligent, organized, and very good with people. I put him in a room with a small team of people to plan a piece of the project. I went in afterward to help him enter all of his data off the network diagram into the software. My role was to read him the activity information (activity description, duration, activity manager, predecessor, successor, etc.) from the network diagram so he could then replicate it in the software. I began to analyze the network while he was entering the data that I called out, and it just didn't make sense to me, but I hadn't been in the planning session. So I said, "I've read the descriptions and how each task was sequenced, but it doesn't make any sense to me. Can you tell me what the conversation was and why these activities were laid out this way?"

He stared at the network diagram, and I could tell I had put him on the spot, so I said, "Let me continue with the data entry while you try to recall the conversation." About ten minutes later, I asked him if he could now explain why the tasks were laid out the way they were, and he said, "No, I don't remember." Either he didn't have the technical expertise to understand the big picture or he didn't follow the discussion closely enough to assemble it all in his head to see the big picture. When you don't understand the big picture, you can't ask good questions of the team. You can't ask, "Why does this have to happen here in order for that to happen over there? Didn't you say you needed to test this before that task could happen? Isn't this part of testing?"

Whenever I finish planning a project, I may not be able to perform any of the activities in the plan because I don't have the technical expertise required, but I do understand how it all fits together and why the tasks are sequenced in a specific way. I understand the big picture. If my employees cannot explain why certain activities are tied together in a specific sequence and describe the project to me as a whole (at least the part they facilitated), they won't work at PSI for long. Project managers have to be able to answer what happens next and why. Otherwise, they're just regurgitating data.

# WHAT TO LOOK FOR IN A PROJECT MANAGER
## PROJECT MANAGERS WHO SEE THE BIG PICTURE

Whether the project manager comes from inside or outside of the organization, they have to understand the big-picture view of the project. They have to understand how every piece of the project works together.

The project manager should be mentally building the project as the planning takes place, so that at the end of the planning session they understand better than anybody else in the room how everything fits together. While this person may not have the technical expertise to carry out each activity personally, they have to understand the big picture well enough to ask great questions. They have to know when to ask how a person can do activity X if activity Y hasn't been finished, or why procurement isn't the owner of a task versus the engineer currently taking responsibility, or point out that legal approvals appear to be missing (or ask if they're needed). Even though the project manager might not understand how each activity physically works, they have a big-picture view of how each activity works toward achieving the end goal.

## PROJECT MANAGERS SHOULD LIVE IN THE MIDDLE

The big-picture view is important, but a good project manager will understand the high-level implications of the project in addition to the gory details. They will live in the middle of both.

Big-picture thinkers are strategic thinkers. They see everything from a fifty-thousand-foot perspective. That's how they're comfortable thinking. They see the world in large buckets, so they are very comfortable planning activities that are 60, 80, or 120 days long. This might be your marketing team. On the other side of the spectrum, you have the detail-oriented people—those who want to get really granular, which we call getting "in the weeds." Detail-oriented people want to plan everything to the nth degree. They want to break every activity into one- or two-hour tasks. These are commonly your engineers and technical team members. Neither the big picture nor the detail-oriented point of view alone will ensure project success.

In my classes, I like to tell the following story to drive the point home about big-picture/strategic versus detail-oriented. I always warn them in advance that I'll be playing on some stereotypes and to please not be offended. Then I smile and say, "Although there may be a grain of truth in them." Now as I look into the audience, I point out that all the engineers are sitting together. Why? Because they understand each other. They speak the same technical language, laugh at the same jokes (insert your favorite Dilbert joke here), and have the shared bond of having survived calculus and differential equations in college. Not too far away from them are the folks from IT—because they speak the same language, albeit a different dialect. I then point out that both groups are as far away as possible from the marketing team, and everyone usually laughs because they realize that is exactly what has happened. Now why does this happen so often in my sessions? Because as human beings we seek comfort. We enjoy being around people we understand—people who speak our language (technical or native) and share our perspective.

I first offer an exaggerated version of an engineer's perspective (again with a smile, of course). I look at the marketing person and say, "I don't understand you marketing people. You have your head in the clouds, and you're always talking about strategy and positioning. I know you have a lot of meetings, but what do you actually do? As an engineer, when I go home at the end of the day, I actually got something done that you can see, touch, feel—a design in CAD, code written, or a test completed with documented results. All you guys in marketing do is talk about nebulous things like strategy and have lunch meetings. You eat some really nice lunches but all you do is talk, talk, talk. You don't really get anything tangible done like I do."

Of course, everyone laughs at my portrayal. Now it's my turn to play the role of marketing. "Wow, you don't have a very high opinion of us, do you? Well, you're at least partially right. We discuss strategy and positioning a lot, and we are high-level strategic thinkers because that's what the company needs us to do. But let's be honest. You engineers are so far down in the weeds that you can't see where you're going. You need somebody like us to give you direction, so you don't fall off the cliff or run into the wall."

> Every project manager must live somewhere in the middle, able to communicate and work with both big-picture and detail-oriented team members.

The truth of the matter is that we need both perspectives. Assuming you are part of a for-profit corporation, making money is one of your goals. However, if engineering is developing products that marketing can't sell, you're not making money. If marketing is selling products that engineering can't build, you're not making money. This is an important role for project management. We need to pull the people that live in the clouds down a little bit and pull the people that are down in the weeds up a little bit so they can exist on the same plane while they are talking about a project.

Every project manager must live somewhere in the middle, able to communicate and work with both big-picture and detail-oriented team members. Living in the middle is an important skill set to develop, and the Project Success Method can help with it.

## PROJECT MANAGERS WITH LEADERSHIP SKILLS

I joined PSI in 1994, and in 2005 I had the privilege of buying the company. Shortly thereafter we brought on a new human resources manager named Stacey. The company was growing, so we were discussing the need to hire some additional staff.

She asked, "Who am I looking for?"

I said, very deadpan, "It's easy. We want engineers with social skills who are willing to travel three weeks a month. Good luck with that."

I always joke that the reason PSI has never had more than twenty-five consultants is because we have already found everyone that met the criteria I gave Stacey. But in all seriousness, the description I gave Stacey wasn't a joke. We hire engineers with social skills because they need to be able to communicate with all different types of personalities on a project. They need to be able to stand in front of a room full of people—some of whom they may know, but many more they may not—and effectively lead the meeting. They need to be good communicators who can ask the right questions—the questions that help the team lay out an effective plan for the project. Of course, part of communication is listening—to information about both the project and the person. In essence, a good project manager needs to have leadership skills—the ability to take control of a room full of people you don't know and get the team moving in the right direction toward a common goal while being the arbiter along the way.

It's very helpful if these leaders either have a background in facilitation or natural facilitation skills. Facilitation is the art of helping a team follow the process in small, manageable chunks so that its members aren't overwhelmed. It's also helping resolve conflicts between individual team members and/or helping individuals get past an obstacle they can't seem to solve on their own. It's really difficult to do this if you've never managed a project before, which is why the majority of people who work for us have an average of more than thirty-five years of postcollege work experience.

One advantage to hiring an outside entity such as PSI to act as a facilitator is that they don't have a hidden agenda. They don't have any preconceived notions about how the project should go, which direction it should go in, or how it should move. They are completely neutral and strictly want to help move the project in a way that benefits the company and leads to a quality, on-time completion date. Since they aren't part of the organization, they don't have to worry about politics. They can concentrate 100 percent on the project. But more on that later.

Finally, project managers should be open-minded. They can't be hell-bent on going left or going right. This can be challenging when a project manager has deep technical knowledge or experience in a particular area of the project. An engineer, for example, that is now taking on the role of a project manager is used to doing things one way, theirs, and may have a hard time understanding or listening to how and why that activity might work another way on that particular project. Good project managers are truly open-minded and able to think of the bigger picture. They strictly want to help move the project in a way that benefits the company and leads to a successful completion.

## PROJECT MANAGERS WHO CAN GET A PROJECT OUT OF THE DITCH

We work with a very wide range of companies, from highly technical (semiconductor, heavy equipment) to some of the best marketing companies in the world, and they all need to execute highly complex, cross-functional projects. And that's where we come in because we are able to help on both ends of the spectrum. It's even more true when I work with technical people (or those with a math or numbers focus). In my live training, we use several cases to reinforce the material. Invariably, as we go through the solution set, someone asks the question, "Is there an optimal solution?" As an engineer myself, I certainly understand where they're coming from. They are used to needing three, four, or five-plus decimal places of accuracy in their daily jobs. And if I'm driving across a bridge they designed or in a vehicle they designed, I *want* them to use five or more decimal places of accuracy. But when it comes to project management, we don't need that level of accuracy. You're just trying to get the ball rolling in the right direction and keep it out of the ditch! It's okay if it drifts a little left or a little right, as long as it stays out of the ditch.

> "Individual commitment to a group effort—that is what makes a team work, a company work, a society work, a civilization work."
>
> —Vince Lombardi

When I was at Georgia Tech, one of the required classes was dynamics. I hadn't particularly enjoyed the prerequisite class on statics, which is the study of forces on a stationary object, so I knew I wouldn't like dynamics, which is the study of the forces on an object in motion. On the first day of class, the professor announced, "They call me the Bamboo Shaft. Look left, look right because two of you won't pass my class." Needless to say, I dropped the class and took it later with a different professor. I later heard a story from one of my friends that stayed in the class that I appreciate to this day. He told me that on one of the last tests before the final a student was pleading his case that he didn't deserve the zero he'd been assigned because the answer was correct—only the sign was wrong. Each time the professor would reply, "But you're wrong." Finally, after several rounds, the frustrated professor said, "You are not a child. If you design a bridge and use the wrong sign, people die. Sit down." And he's right. Some jobs do require that level of accuracy, but project management usually isn't one of them.

After attending the Project Success Method training, project managers are excited to implement the techniques they've learned but for some reason want to wait on a new, pristine project rather than one that is already "in flight." I strongly disagree. There's no reason not to use it on the in-flight project. At PSI we often get parachuted into projects that are well underway but have fallen into the ditch. When I say *fallen into the ditch*, I mean that the projects are off schedule with no line of sight to get them back on track. This often happens when team members work in a silo, which is a by-product of normal project management. When we're pulling projects out of the ditch, we stick to our process, just as we do when starting a project from scratch. Nothing changes. We still write charters and develop work breakdown structures and network diagrams with the whole team. We take every step that I outlined in the Project Success Method in chapter 1.

Interestingly, whenever I tell a project manager who needs help getting out of the ditch that we need to write a charter for the project, they always say, "No, we don't need to waste time writing a charter. The team has been working on this thing for six months. Everybody knows what has to be done."

I always smile and say, "No problem. Give me thirty minutes with the team so I can understand the project before we move into planning."

Every time, we end up taking the full three to four hours I'd asked for to write the charter because if there are fifteen people on the team, there are fifteen different opinions on the project; no one ever got them together and had a conversation about what the project is *and isn't*.

## PROJECT MANAGERS WHO KNOW WHEN TO SAY NO

I got a call from a client about three months before the Sochi Olympics started. He said, "Hey, we're over here in Sochi, Russia, for the Winter Olympics, and the hotels are not ready. Can you come over and help us?"

I said, "I can come over, and we'll build a plan that shows you're not going to make it, but with three months left, there's probably no way to fix this. There's simply not enough time." And I was right, the hotels were either not completed or were of very poor quality (a quick Google search shows some very disturbing stories complete with pictures).

Good project managers know they need to be brutally honest at times. They know when the people calling for the project need to be told that their expectations are unrealistic. In the Sochi hotel example, they were able to finish the hotels as the result of a mandate from the highest levels of the Russian government that had people working around the clock to get them built, but they were terribly done. This is a perfect example of how quality is affected when you push too hard to meet a deadline: the quality lever goes down and the cost lever goes up, just like it did in the three-hour house example we described in Chapter 3.

Large sporting events certainly aren't the only place where brutal honesty is called for. Many companies "overlaunch." They launch project after project without giving any real thought to how much they already have on their plate, and they unrealistically hope everything will get done. And since project managers are usually afraid to say no to upper management, they say, "I'll try" and end up failing. The project either gets killed after they've spent too many resources (people and/or money), or it is delivered late with quality negatively impacted. Projects need prioritization. Someone needs to say, "We are doing this project first, this one second, and if we have the resources, this one third." Of course, at large corporations the projects can number in the hundreds, but the prioritization still needs to happen. Unfortunately, many companies either don't know how to do this or purposely ignore it, "hoping" it will all get done.

Someone on the team will often say, "You know, Clint, we're complaining about the deadline always being unrealistic, but the truth is that we always make it." When I investigate that statement, I usually find one of two things happened enabling them to hit the deadline. They either worked eighty-plus hours a week, which is simply not sustainable in the long run, or they did indeed hit the date—with something. Was the quality they promised at the beginning of the project actually delivered? Absolutely not! The full-color video documentation ends up being black-and-white photocopies instead. The training that was supposed to take place prior to the rollout of the new HR system is performed after the rollout is complete. Or even worse, the product is shipped with known bugs/flaws. The quality was sacrificed in order to hit the date.

## PROJECT MANAGERS WHO AREN'T AFRAID TO KILL PROJECTS

Sometimes the most successful project is the one you don't do. One of our clients provides a great example of this. When we arrived, their projects were being killed at a fairly high rate, which is neither good nor bad. The problem was the timing of the kills. The projects being killed had typically exhausted all of the resource allocation and most of the budget and were already at or beyond the desired finish date. After fully embracing and implementing the Project Success Method, they now are able to make intelligent decisions to kill a project within the first one to two weeks. This allows them to redirect those resources to other projects where there is a higher likelihood of success. The cost savings are significant if you are able to save twelve-plus months of a fifteen-person team's time. Even at a fully burdened rate per person of only $100,000 per year, they're saving $1.5 million by killing that project early!

From a team perspective, project managers must be able to get a team member who's been diligently working on a project that needs to be killed to accept the project's fate.

A team member who has invested a significant amount of time over the last six or nine months doesn't want to see that work wasted. That team member has ownership of the project and wants to see the thing through or, at the very least, see that work shelved in a way that it will be used in some capacity on another project. The common argument you need to be ready for is "We should go ahead and finish it, so we'll have something we can put to use later." But do we really want to waste another six months or even six weeks on a bad project? Of course not—but it's human nature to want to see it through.

We need to approach the topic of killing the project with care and understanding. A project manager who says, "Listen, we're shutting it down. It doesn't matter what you think. The decision has been made" risks losing that team member's commitment on future projects. This is risky since that project manager will likely work with that person again. And once someone has a bad experience working for a project manager, that manager's project becomes the team member's lowest priority, or worse.

Good project managers clearly articulate why a project is no longer needed. They may say something like, "Listen, your work on this project was invaluable. We really couldn't have gotten as far as we did without you. We're going to put it on the shelf, and hopefully we can leverage this later on in a different project. You're so valuable to us that we really can't afford to waste your talent on another three months of this project, which isn't going anywhere. We want to use you on four other projects that are going to give us a chance to make millions of dollars."

This approach helps the team member understand that the company currently has other projects with a greater chance for success and that their work will hopefully get repurposed in a future project, not wasted. Of course, this can all be avoided if we can kill a project early, before the team gets too invested. In fact, with one of our clients we were killing almost 30 percent of the projects immediately after planning because it was obvious the team couldn't meet the project requirements. That's a huge win! All of those resources got redeployed immediately to other projects that could be successful rather than languishing on bad projects.

Unhappy team members don't do high-quality work because they don't have ownership or buy into you or your projects. If they don't like you or at least respect you, you become their lowest priority.

## IT'S ALL ABOUT THE TEAM

How you engage with your team greatly influences your success because they are the ones actually executing the project. You must involve the team in the process from the very beginning. Team members should participate in every phase of the process—developing the charter, work breakdown structure, and network diagram, as well as the project control sessions. This engagement ensures you have their commitment and buy-in. After all, when you work in a matrix, the only chance you have to be successful is if the team members "own" their activities, meaning they hold themselves accountable for getting their tasks done. They must feel like it's *their* project—not yours.

## DON'T MANDATE, ASK

One way to drive commitment and buy-in at the team member level, which is where it belongs, is to *ask* rather than mandate. Don't assign someone to a task. Ask who is the responsible person and let them accept it by saying, "That's my task. I own it. Put my name on it." You've probably heard someone say they're afraid to leave the room because if they do their name gets assigned to everything. Well, our process ensures that doesn't happen. Our rule is that the person must be in the room and accept responsibility. No one else can assign your name to a task as the activity manager but you. The same goes for durations. Only the person who has accepted responsibility for a task can give the duration. That's how you drive accountability!

## UNDERSTAND THE DIFFERENCE BETWEEN THE CORE TEAM AND RESOURCES

We must make a distinction between what we call the core team and project resources. The core team is the group of stakeholders invested in the project. Activity managers, for example, are part of the core team. Activity managers make sure each activity gets done. They put their names on the individual activities and take ownership of those tasks. Then they utilize the available resources to make sure those activities get done. These resources can be internal company employees or external contractors and vendors.

The resources are the people (or equipment, materials, space/access, information, money, etc.) who physically do the work or are consumed doing the work. They do the physical design, they type the code, and they dig the ditch. In most projects, the number of resources far outweighs the number of core team members. The project manager must know the difference between the two and how they function within the team. The resources, for example, do not need to be involved in every meeting. Their time is often better spent doing the actual work. When the project manager wants to know the status, he or she asks the activity manager, not the resources. This minimizes the overhead on the resources so their productivity can be maximized.

## GET EVERYONE ON THE SAME PAGE

For us, getting every team member on the same page starts by developing a charter. As I mentioned earlier, a project charter ensures that every project stakeholder knows what's expected of the project. It also protects the team from scope creep and other disasters that can happen when stakeholders have different expectations.

For the charter process to work, everyone—marketing, IT, design, everyone—must achieve consensus on where the project is headed. If a charter is written, and a key department, like marketing, is missing, they may create an unsalable product. Similarly, if engineering isn't present, they may devise a campaign to sell an unbuildable widget. An organization that wants to make money must plan collaboratively.

About ten years ago, we began working with a company in Silicon Valley. Brad was the project manager on one of our first projects there. As he tells it, he was a bit reluctant to be the guinea pig, but his fears were quickly allayed.

While we were writing the charter for the project—a chip for an automotive application—it became clear that the deadline for chip delivery was aggressive. The internal customer,[6] a marketing director, was in the room and made the comment "Oh, by the way, I've told the

---

6    Projects are often completed for internal customers, whose job is to turn around and deliver or sell to the external customer or consumer.

customer this chip will be ASIL D compliant." ASIL D compliancy is a standard that the automobile industry uses.

As soon as he said that, the rest of the team said, "Well, stop right there. This is already a very aggressive timeline. There's no way we can make this chip ASIL D compliant in that time frame. Plus, that standard hasn't even been finalized yet. It's still in development. There's no way we can add new functionality to support this standard."

After a thirty-minute dialogue, the marketing director agreed the chip would not be ASIL D compliant. This was written in the charter and signed by the internal customer. From that moment on, Brad was sold on our process. He saw the value of getting everyone on the same page and having it in writing. Human memories are faulty. Brad realized that it wasn't out of the realm of possibility that without the charter, six weeks later the marketing director could have said, "But I thought we agreed the chip would be ASIL D compliant."

## GET ALL THE RIGHT PEOPLE IN THE SAME ROOM

Years ago, we did some work for one of the major movie studios in Hollywood. Our task was to help a team developing an app for kids that was targeted to be released in conjunction with its associated movie launch. As we were developing the charter, someone raised a question, the answer to which would have a significant impact on the length and cost of the project. Unfortunately, no one in the room knew the answer. It turns out we were missing a team member. Nobody from marketing was in the room to answer the question "How many languages are we going to release the app in?" To effectively plan a project, we need to ensure that all required functional areas are represented.

A project manager who fails to get the right people in the room will end up planning a project that won't work. Missing any key player will narrow the sense of the project's scope. Only inviting marketing brings a marketing-only perspective. Only inviting engineering brings an engineering-only perspective. Are legal contracts involved? If so, do we need someone on the team from legal? How about supply chain or HR? You need to engage all parties.

Of course, there is an exception to every rule. There are a few select people you *do not want* in the planning session. For example, years ago we had just started helping a client plan a project, when the external customer, the one who would actually buy the product, walked into the room. Planning sessions are meant to be a safe haven for open discussion, dialogue, and even arguments. They're designed for the team to talk about the issues, warts, and the things that haven't gone well in the past. These honest conversations are not ones you want to have if your end user is sitting in the room. So, while you want your team in the room, leave the external customer out of it. Of course, we'll share the final plan with them and solicit their feedback, but they don't need to see how the sausage gets made—they just want to enjoy the final product!

> "Teamwork is the ability to work together toward a common vision. The ability to direct individual accomplishments toward organizational objectives. It is the fuel that allows common people to attain uncommon results."
>
> —Andrew Carnegie

The reason we start our process by getting everyone in the same room is that it intentionally removes every person who will work on the project from their silo. As I mentioned earlier, when I teach the Project Success Method to a class of fifty people, for example, engineers and marketers keep their distance from one another. That dynamic doesn't change when they exit the classroom and move into the actual planning of the project. In fact, it likely is more pronounced, but to develop a collaborative plan, you have to force people out of their silos. This is why at the beginning of every project we get the core team in the same room for a three-day planning session.

## WHY FACE-TO-FACE TEAM BUILDING MATTERS

The average person on a project team has worked with other people on his or her team for years, yet many probably can't describe what their teammates look like. Why? Because historically every interaction that team member has had with his or her teammates has been done virtually through email, chat, IM, or other collaboration tool.

Getting the entire team into one room for a multiday planning session encourages team members to develop real relationships with each other. It also removes many of the obstacles that get in the way of effective project management, particularly excuses from team members who claim they didn't know about or understand something because they weren't part of the planning process.

When everyone plans together, you get ownership among the entire team for the project plan and mission. Once all the pieces are agreed upon, and everybody has buy-in, the team moves toward the same goal rather than running off in different directions.

This is incredibly valuable for the team members and the project. Even if a team member had nothing to offer during the charter and planning session, they heard the conversations that took place. So they understand why something is in, or out of, scope and why activities are sequenced in a specific way.

When we first started working with the Silicon Valley company, they'd been planning projects for years and years but in a very ad hoc way. Everyone had their own way of managing things, and the process was inconsistent, as were the results. In a typical design project, the person who designs a chip cannot also be the person who tests it. Naturally, the designer knows how the chip design works and would be biased if they were the one testing it. You want someone who is completely independent and has had nothing to do with that design to test the chip. So these two engineers work independently of each other, even though their work is very much tied together.

We brought the project team together in a room for three days to plan a project. During one of the sessions, the design engineer and the test engineer, who had been working together for seven years virtually but had never actually met before, were having a sidebar conversation while another part of the team was actively planning its part of the project. The test engineer said to the design engineer, "You know, if you had made one small change to your design, it could have saved 30 percent of my test time."

That conversation could have happened anytime during the past seven years, but it didn't until the two engineers were in a room face-to-face. When projects are planned in silos or virtually, these conversations are missed. These potentially powerful time and cost savings go by the wayside. It's only when you gather people together in a room in a collaborative way that these things bubble to the top.

## TECHNOLOGY IS NOT THE ANSWER

We've talked about how even though technology is a tool to leverage on a project, it's not the answer to successful project management. I've worked with teams who have tried to substitute internet-based meetings on platforms such as Zoom for face-to-face meetings. While these platforms can occasionally help bridge multiple time zones, they aren't overly effective. The nature of them allows team members to continue working on their computer, check their phones, or give in to a million other distractions when they're supposed to be listening to important project updates.

As this is going to print, the world is in the throes of a global pandemic. For the last five-plus months, many of us have been forced to work remotely. Physical face-to-face meetings are strongly discouraged and technology has supported our virtual isolation. Some might think that this recent experience has changed my mind on the benefits of face-to-face planning sessions. To the contrary, my views have been reinforced. Research is already showing that Zoom fatigue is a "thing" and not a long-term substitute for face-to-face meetings. There is anxiety caused by screen glitches and freezes, along with the occasional audio silence— "Was it intended or am I frozen again?" I've even seen it mentioned that it's stressful for some of us to stare at our face on the screen. I didn't see that one coming, but it makes sense. We don't know our collar is out of whack and our hair is mussed in face-to-face meetings; we just assume we look good. In one of our planning sessions, it's common to have twenty to twenty-five attendees. In a meeting room, I have no difficulty "seeing" everyone even through my peripheral vision, and I am able to hone in on unexpected behavior. That is not the case in virtual meetings. With so many small frames, it is not possible to "see" with the same detail. Plus, many only have their profile photo displayed. In both cases, I am unable to see fingers drumming, feet tapping, or other nervous tics. (Full disclosure: it is easier to recognize who is talking when their frame is highlighted ... especially when you don't recognize everyone's voices yet.)

As I mentioned, side conversations can be powerful and add tremendous value. A typical three-day planning session offers three lunches, at least one team dinner, and six to twelve coffee breaks for these conversations to take place, not to mention the time over continental breakfast and after the session officially ends at the end of each day. These conversations happen organically when face-to-face. They simply do not happen when working remotely.

Finally, something I've long recognized about myself is that I'm a touchy-feely people person—perhaps an anomaly for an electrical engineer—but I was reminded of this fact by a recent article in Fast Company about a six-foot office. Cushman & Wakefield, a commercial real estate company, has developed this six-foot concept in their Amsterdam headquarters. "The core premise is to ensure that six feet ... stays between people at all times. This behavior is encouraged through properly spaced desks, but also visual signals, such as a circle embedded in the carpeting around each desk to ensure people don't get too close."[7] I actually shuddered when I read the article. I thought to myself, "Is that what the future looks like? A world where I only see my colleagues as germ-carrying, pathogen delivery vehicles." That is not the world I want to work in. While I certainly hope that better air filtration systems are developed, and people realize it's okay to work from home when they're sick, I hope we come back to a sense of normalcy where Joe is neither merely viewed as an email address or a virus carrier but as a living breathing human being I have a connection to and relationship with. Part of being human is the need to belong to a tribe. The same holds true in project work. We succeed as a team or fail as individuals. I truly believe that.

## HOW TO DESIGN AND LEAD EFFECTIVE PROJECT PLANNING AND CONTROL MEETINGS

We've all seen projects fall apart because the project managers were bullies. They didn't connect to their team, didn't listen to them, and didn't respect them as people. I remember one instance where, regardless of what was going on in the project, the project manager's main goal seemed to be to find someone on his team to belittle.

---

7    Mark Wilson, "Our offices will never be the same after COVID-19. Here's what they could look like," Fast Company, April 13, 2020, https://www.fastcompany.com/90488060/our-offices-will-never-be-the-same-after-covid-19-heres-what-they-could-look-like.

During every planning session, this project manager would single someone out and ask leading questions that were designed to make the person look stupid. He'd say, "Well, Steve, don't you think we should go left on this?"

And when Steve would say, "Yeah, I think we should go left," he'd tell Steve what an idiot he was for thinking that. It was brutal. This project manager made enemies during every project. I never understood how he thought this approach would be helpful. When a project slips (when the plan is delayed beyond the deadline), which happens constantly during the life of a project, the people on your team are the only ones who can get the project back on track. After all, they are the ones that have to agree to stay late or work weekends or rearrange their priorities (delay their work on other projects) in order to remove the lateness on your project. So, what is the advantage of making enemies? The more people dislike you, the less likely it is that they're going to do what you're asking of them. I call this punitive project management, and in the end everyone suffers—the team, the project manager, and the project itself—as a result of it.

## PUNITIVE PROJECT MANAGEMENT

Early in my PSI career I was in a compression session, where we were as a team trying to compress the project back to meet our target deadline.

When we took a break, I started talking to one of the guys on the team. Shaking his head, he said, "You're doing all this work to get your plan back to the deadline, but even if you do that, you're still going to be late."

I said, "First of all, it's not my plan; it's your plan. You guys put it together; I just replicated it in the software." (For the record, it is never a good omen of their commitment and buy-in when a team member refers to the plan as "yours" and not "ours.") "Why would we still be late? We have all the steps laid out in the right sequence and with the correct durations. If we're able to compress it back to the target date, we should be good."

Then he said, "Well, because they don't have all the right durations." I was confused until he said, "I'm one of the people on the back end of the critical path, and right now I've been given ten days for my task."

An alarm bell went off when he told me he'd been "given" a duration. I knew immediately that he hadn't had any say in what that duration should be, which probably contributed significantly to his earlier reference to "your" plan. As we continued talking, he shared that he knew he probably needed thirty days to finish his task. Then he said, "But I'm not going to tell the project manager." He must have seen the confusion on my face because he smiled and said, "I've worked with this person before, and I know for a fact that if I tell him today that I need thirty days for a task he's given me ten days for, he's going to make my life a living hell for the next six months," (which was when the task was scheduled to start). "Instead," he continued, "six months from now, on day ten of my task, instead of saying, 'I'm done,' I'm going to announce that I need four more weeks. I'm saving myself six months of grief."

This is punitive project management. And no one wins in the end. The team member gets a reputation for not being forthcoming. The project ultimately fails because the bad news is received too late to recover from since the task is at the latter part of the critical path. The project manager has failed to deliver the project successfully. Why? Two reasons. First, he assigned activities and durations with no input from the person ultimately performing the task, so they felt no overwhelming obligation to complete it. Second, the project manager created an environment in which the truth was not acceptable.

After working on projects for almost thirty years, negative examples like these have taught me that project management should be helpful, collaborative, and promote commitment, not be punitive.

## ORGANIZE THE DEBATE

The facilitator of a planning session has to engage everyone in the conversation. Say I have twenty people in a room. Typically, two or three people will naturally do all the talking. These people tend to be strong-willed individuals who are very opinionated. They think they know the most about the project, and sometimes they do, but if they go unchecked, they will dominate the conversation.

So how do you get the other eighteen people involved? You look for nonverbal cues that can open a debate. When I'm facilitating, I look for the person who grimaces, rolls their eyes, or whispers in a seatmate's ear when someone else says something. This body language indicates disagreement, and when I see it, I'll say, "I'm not sure everybody agrees with that last statement."

Then I'll ask one of the people who gave a nonverbal cue for an opinion. I never call anyone out for obviously not agreeing, but I do ask for feedback. My goal is to get input from all twenty people; as the facilitator, it's my job to draw out as many opinions as I can.

## KEEP YOUR COOL

I've never seen a hot-headed team leader rally a group of people behind them. At least not in a positive way. The thing about project management is that not only does the project manager have to stay cool during stressful situations, but he or she also needs to be the calming force within the team.

I've been in plenty of situations where two people on the team get into it. Sometimes the argument occurs between two high-level team members. The project manager has to be comfortable stepping into that situation and calming it down, listening to one person talk, giving the other person a chance to talk, identifying the conflict, and helping both parties reach a resolution.

It's important to note that you will rarely get everyone to fully agree. That would be ideal but isn't realistic. Instead, we strive for group consensus, which we'll discuss in Chapter 7.

## APPOINT A FACILITATOR

Ideally, your planning facilitator should *never* be your project manager. They have very different personalities. Project managers tend to be type A personalities who are constantly driving things to completion, whereas facilitators need to be more inclusive and collaborative. Project managers tend to be those people who dominate the conversation. They have a lot of expertise, and their job is to get the project done, but when the project is being planned, you need to hear from everyone. Instead of having a project manager facilitate, ask someone who is not on the project team but is versed in the planning process to facilitate. Offer to reciprocate on that person's next project. Why? As an outside consultant filling the role of a facilitator, I have no hidden agenda. I don't care if the project goes left or right. I only care that the PSM process is being followed (the charter is written with the team, the work breakdown structure is developed by the team members responsible, etc.). If the facilitator is also a team member, they may either have or be perceived to have a hidden agenda. To avoid even the suggestion of impropriety, we suggest the facilitator not be a member of that project team. If your organization is small and you have to choose a team member to act as the facilitator, then I suggest it not be the project manager, as we explain in the next paragraph.

Your facilitator should be a good listener. After all, their job is to extract data from the team members while resolving conflicts between them. The facilitator tries to do each of the things I just talked about: engage people, not let one or two people dominate the conversation, achieve consensus. Project managers don't intentionally do this, but their job is to push, push, push, so when they facilitate, even the most well-intentioned of them will typically fall back into their comfort zone and dominate the conversation. Very quickly, there's only one person talking—the project manager—and they are basically writing the charter for the project, so it becomes their charter, not the team's charter. They've missed the first opportunity they had to include the team and begin to foster the bonds between them.

## HAVE AN AGENDA

Before your planning or control session, set an agenda and do not deviate from it. People need to know the structure of the meeting. They need to know the meeting will start on time, how the meeting will be organized, and what will be talked about in what order, every single time. Hopefully, this will prevent someone from hijacking the meeting or going off on some tangent that should be addressed elsewhere.

Facilitators need to silence meeting hijackers. They need to table whatever issue is sidetracking forward movement. Meetings frequently get hijacked after the planning session during one of the control meetings. As you remember, control meetings are the update meetings, ideally lasting less than an hour, that occur throughout the life of the project either every week or every other week. Each control meeting looks at the project plan, which is static, and makes the course corrections to true it up. These meetings are intended to update your plan to reflect what has actually happened since the last update. We know what was supposed to happen, but what actually did happen? What do we need to add that we didn't know about before? What durations need changing? What start and finish dates need changing? Once you plug all of this new information back into your plan, the plan is correct, accurate, and reflects reality again. Unfortunately, these updates almost always result in slippage.

The first part of a control meeting is updating. The second and much more difficult part is making up for these missed deadlines, or slippage. If a project slips by two weeks, the control meeting helps determine how to get those two weeks back. You do that by manipulating the critical path and making decisions regarding what could change. This conversation always opens up the risk of hijacking because the people in the room are problem solvers. They want to solve project issues rather than look at scheduling issues. This is an extremely easy trap to fall into and must be avoided. If you allow this to happen, the meeting becomes a design review, focused on product or project issues rather than schedule issues.

As the facilitator, you have to remind people that solving project or product issues is not the point of the control meeting. This meeting is about addressing schedule issues, understanding where the project is today, making the schedule accurate, and removing any slippage. As the facilitator, you need to be strict when you see this happen and say, "You guys are trying to solve a design issue, and that's not what we are here to do right now. We'll add an activity to the plan to solve that issue, but let's refocus and concentrate on solving the schedule issues."

The team needs to know that control meetings are going to be short, succinct, and to the point. The meeting won't exceed an hour, and team members will leave knowing how the schedule has changed to account for slippage. Then they can go back to their jobs and execute the changes they've agreed to in order to resolve the schedule slippage.

By the way, while I recommend the facilitator during planning not be the project manager, once the update and control sessions begin, it is fairly typical for the project manager to assume the facilitation role.

---

## SAMPLE CONTROL MEETING AGENDA

Ten minutes: Issue collection. The project manager asks the team what issues they want to discuss. The issues are listed, typically on a flip chart, and then tabled until the end of the control meeting.

Fifteen minutes: Activity update. The project manager goes into the plan and updates activities based on the status given to him or her by the activity managers.

Twenty-five minutes: Validation and compression. The team validates the plan, makes sure the new durations and activities are correct, and compresses any slippage out of the plan.

Ten minutes: Issue resolution. The project manager revisits the flip chart. Anyone who didn't add an issue to the chart or isn't part of the resolution is free to leave the meeting.

---

## BE RESPECTFUL OF YOUR TEAM MEMBERS' TIME

Keeping to a strict agenda also respects your team members' time. They know that if you say you need them in a meeting for an hour, they won't return to their desk one and a half hours later. Team members will also appreciate agendas that end with issue resolution because if they didn't bring up an issue or are not part of the resolution, they can leave and get back to the many tasks they're working on.

This is not death by PowerPoint. This meeting is laser focused on updating the schedule and resolving slippage. It's not a design review, and the project manager will not allow the meeting to be hijacked. People like getting things done and not having their time wasted. Everyone on your team is really busy already, so remember to keep your meetings short and helpful. Your team will show their appreciation by actually showing up!

## BE RESPECTFULLY AUTHORITATIVE

Project management is difficult for numerous reasons, one being that it is a balancing act. Project managers have to listen but also be authoritative. When I first started working at PSI, I was overseeing a planning session for a Caterpillar project. I was already a little nervous. I'd been working at Coca-Cola, where I felt comfortable, and had just moved over to a new industry. I was in my early thirties at the time and had a team of about twenty-five people, several of whom had thirty-plus years of experience, to guide through the planning process. As the meeting was kicking off, one of those thirty-plus year guys asked me how old I was. When I told him I was thirty-two, he smiled and said, "Son, I've been doing my job longer than you've been alive. What could you possibly tell me?"

I could have lost the team at that point, but instead of fumbling over my words in an attempt to justify my value, I said, "I'm not here to tell you how to do your job. You're already the expert at what you do, and I'm glad you're here because we need your expertise to deliver this project by the deadline. I'm here to facilitate the process of getting your expertise, along with everyone else's, captured in a project plan that you all agree with and are committed to." I let that team member know that I wasn't there to take his job or outsmart him. I was there to bring together the collective expertise in the room in order to get the project done. Consequently, I didn't lose control of the room.

Project managers have to be authoritative. While you are certainly going to be collaborative and do a lot of listening, at the end of the day it's your responsibility to deliver the project successfully—so you are in charge! In the navy, we called this military bearing.

## EARN AND MAINTAIN THE TRUST OF YOUR TEAM

Earning and maintaining the trust of your team can be quite difficult. The first project you'll work on with your team will be the toughest because they won't trust you yet. As I've mentioned before, most people come to project management with the expectation of pain. They've only ever seen project management used one way: the punitive way, in which they are constantly hounded to reach deadlines that don't work for them because they had no input or are micromanaged and told they have do this task from eight o'clock to eight fifteen and that task from eight thirty to nine thirty. They have no flexibility. People who have experienced this type of project management won't believe you—at least not initially—when you say your project will be kinder and gentler and, ultimately, all about them.

During that initial planning session, expect pushback. Your team will tell you over and over that your process won't work despite the fact they haven't experienced it yet. However, at the end of a three-day planning session, they'll be converts. They'll go from "this will never work here—we're different" to "we should plan all of our projects like this." This happens to us all the time. During training I often hear, "This won't work in our organization." Inevitably, after they've participated in an actual planning session for their project, the biggest resisters become our greatest converts. This change in attitude is largely driven by the human element of project planning. When projects are planned using the Project Success Method, people matter. Their opinions count when project scope is being determined; durations and activities are constructed around their availability and commitment; by spending time together as a team for three days, they start to know and respect their teammates. This encourages a collaborative process that cannot be achieved with a process that is not people focused.

Once your team sees how planning will help them and that project management doesn't have to be painful, they will start to trust you. But that first project is always the hardest one because there's always fear and trepidation. No one will believe that project management can be used in a nonpunitive, helpful way because they've never experienced that.

One of our clients filmed the planning session for one of their projects. It's a great video that shows the entire Project Success Method planning process in action—on an actual project being planned by real people, not actors—condensed down to four minutes. I love this video for several reasons. One, it's phenomenal to watch the team members interact and have conversations about the project and their roles in it. Not once during the video do you see a single person working alone. It's always done with someone else. The collaboration piece is incredible to see. The second reason I love this video is that at the end of the video, when the team plugs the final compression change into the software, and the software shows that the project will meet the deadline, the room erupts into applause. Finally, I think the last line of the video sums up the people side perfectly by stating, "We begin the session as individuals and finish the project as a team." That's really what our collaborative project planning process does. It forces people out of silos so they can form relationships, establish mutual accountability, and succeed as a team on whatever project they're working on.

## CHAPTER 4 KEY TAKEAWAYS

- Project managers need to be unbiased, with no hidden agenda, and understand the big picture.

- Selecting project managers from within the organization can provide the project with a level of tribal knowledge that is unattainable by hiring external project managers.

- Hiring project managers who are not associated with your company can bring a new perspective that internal project managers may not be able to offer.

- Project managers have to have the ability to communicate with both high-level strategic thinkers and detail-oriented team members.

- Project managers have to be good communicators who can do these things:
  - kill a project as soon as possible
  - get the project out of the ditch by bringing the team together and following the process

- ask for the team's input rather than dictate

- leverage core team members for planning and control rather than the resources

- Face-to-face chartering, planning, and team building are vitally important to project management because they get everyone on the same page, result in a written agreement for the project that all parties can reference, and drive team member commitment.

- Effective planning sessions include an agenda, organized debate, the right attendees, and a neutral facilitator (ideally not the project manager).

- Earning and maintaining the trust of your team is the only way to successfully manage a project that is on time, on budget, and high quality—particularly in a matrix.

- Project managers must keep their cool in all situations and help diffuse conflict between team members.

"Unity is strength . . .
when there is teamwork and
collaboration, wonderful
things can be achieved."

—MATTIE STEPANEK

CHAPTER 5:

# MAKE PEOPLE MATTER

**CONSIDER THIS EXAMPLE:** Cara is working on five projects. For each project Cara interacts with a number of people, typically via email. On one project, Cara's main contact is joe@acmecorporations.com. Every week joe@acmecorporations.com sends Cara emails asking her to do various tasks. If Cara doesn't know Joe—if he's just another email address in a series of email addresses—how committed is she to getting the work done by the deadline she's given? Maybe she deprioritizes his request because she's behind on another project. Since Cara doesn't have a relationship with Joe, she isn't as aware of how her work affects him. She only loosely knows that whatever decisions she makes might have some impact on the nonperson who is joe@acmecorporations.com.

Joe and Cara have worked together for years in this noncollaborative, email-only way. This is how Cara's entire relationship with Joe goes: Joe assigns Cara tasks with due dates, she finishes her tasks (sometimes after the assigned due date), emails them to Joe, Joe does something with them, and eventually the project is complete, and the product hits the marketplace. The company makes money, and everything is great. However, when Cara misses a deadline, she doesn't feel any repercussions. Joe isn't her manager. He's just an email address. So what happens? Because Cara hasn't felt any repercussions for her tardiness, she assumes that being late is acceptable. And it's not that she's lazy; she routinely puts in fifty-plus hour weeks across all five of her projects. She's working hard. If she's not feeling any pain for missing deadlines, she thinks it must be because everyone recognizes that she's being assigned more work than she can reasonably complete. She's simply not aware of the big picture.

What Cara doesn't know is that every time she misses a deadline, Joe has to scramble on his end to make up for the lost time. As a result, Joe has missed numerous important events in his children's lives, like soccer matches, basketball games, and dance recitals. Cara doesn't mean to do this—she's not even aware that it's happening—but these situations occur because Cara doesn't feel accountable to Joe. As a result, Cara doesn't think in terms of how her actions might affect Joe.

> The fact of the matter is, most of us feel disconnected from the project, as though we're working with email addresses, not the people behind them.

Living in a matrix encourages a silo mentality. We sit at our desks, do our work, and answer emails related to five different projects, but who are these emails coming from? People we've never seen or talked to face-to-face. The silo lifestyle means we don't have real relationships with the people we're working with. We've never interacted with them in a meaningful way. And on the off chance that we have met them in person, it was likely only in passing. The fact of the matter is, most of us feel disconnected from the project, as though we're working with email addresses, not the people behind them.

Successful teams operate on the notion that people matter. Every single team member has a name and a face and is responsible and accountable for a task or series of tasks. They all understand that when they lag behind it not only affects their own work, but it also affects the work and personal time of other team members. The first step in making each person on any team matter is to force them to leave their silos, interact with their teammates, and begin to form relationships.

## HOW TO BUILD ACCOUNTABILITY AMONG TEAM MEMBERS

Everyone's been involved in a project that includes receiving an email from someone who says, "Hey, we're starting a new project. You have a five-day task to complete, and it's due in three months." If you're lucky, you might also get a high-level project background statement that briefly describes the project at a cursory level, but the email request and background information isn't enough to truly engage anyone in any project. It's enough information to explain what's happening, but in a very distant way. At this point, how engaged are you in the project? How dedicated to it are you? How much accountability do you feel toward your teammates? Chances are not much.

The best way to engage your team members from day one is to create a sense of accountability among them. Get everyone in the same room together. Using the Project Success Method, plan projects in a collaborative way that forces conversations to take place.

These planning sessions serve several purposes. One of the most important outcomes is that they turn email addresses into living, breathing human beings. Let's go back to Cara and Joe. They work in a matrix, meaning they may also work in different cities or countries. Without a planning session, all Cara knows is that when she's done with her part of an activity, she emails it to Joe. Joe does some magic on his end, and, as I've said, when the project finishes, the company makes money.

If Cara and Joe get to participate in a planning session, they develop a relationship. First, they put a name with a face. Then, they get to know each other, not only during planning but also over breaks, lunches, and team dinners. And as the team collaboratively builds a plan, Cara sees *exactly* how her activities affect Joe's activities *and* how Joe's activities and whether he meets his deadlines or not affect the end date of the project. So during the planning process alone, Cara learns much more about how her work affects Joe and the project as a whole. Now, say that during a coffee break, Cara and Joe start talking. It's just chitchat, but while they're talking, Cara learns that Joe has two kids about the same age as hers and that they are all heavily involved in soccer.

Later, as the planning session continues, Cara is surprised to learn that some of her tasks, including the one that feeds into Joe, are actually on the critical path. Before the planning session, she assumed none of her tasks were on the critical path because no one ever reprimanded her for being late, and she never saw the project end date slip after her task was late. She mentions this to Joe. She says, "I don't understand how I'm on the critical path. I've been late in the past, and the end of the project didn't move out."

That's when Joe says, "Well, that's because I made it up. On our last project, I received your input three days late, but I knew that if I didn't do something, the project was going to be late, so I made it up by working two weekends in a row. The really frustrating part is that I had to miss my oldest daughter's state championship matches that were played those weekends."

Cara feels terrible. She wouldn't want to miss her daughter's soccer match if the situation were reversed. She apologizes to Joe and promises herself that she will do all she can to meet her deadlines from now on. After the kickoff meeting, Cara and Joe return to their respective offices, but something has changed between them—their relationship. Cara still communicates with Joe by email, but when her tasks are due, she has more focus and feels more accountable for getting them done on time. Cara doesn't want Joe to have to work over the weekend or miss some big event in his kid's life because she didn't get her work in on time. Cara and Joe still work together in the same way, yet their dynamic has changed. To Cara, Joe is no longer merely an email address; he is a living, breathing human being who is impacted by her actions. She not only feels accountable to the project and the project manager, she feels accountable to Joe.

## WHAT FACE-TO-FACE COLLABORATION DOES FOR TEAMS

In addition to sealing a bond between team members, face-to-face collaboration also abolishes incorrect assumptions, aids problem solving, and encourages sacrifice.

### FACE-TO-FACE COLLABORATION ABOLISHES INCORRECT ASSUMPTIONS

When project teams do not meet face-to-face for formal planning sessions, everything happens virtually. A lot of one-way communications (emails, texts, Jira posts, etc.) take place, and a lot of assumptions are made. Team members make assumptions about who is doing what, and as a result things are finished late or not at all, and the project slips.

I got an eye-opening lesson in assumptions early in my career that has stuck with me ever since. I was helping a Fortune 100 manufacturer shut down a fifty-year-old manufacturing facility. The company wanted to shut the facility down and move the equipment to several smaller locations across the United States because they were embroiled in a political situation that led the executives to believe shutting the facility down was the best option. When I sat down with the team to develop the charter for the project, we had a long, lively discussion about the project's objectives. When I asked why we were doing the project, the engineers began questioning the prudence of moving equipment and processes that were fifty years old. They wanted to go out and find a better manufacturing process so they wouldn't have to move the antiquated equipment. Their thought was that a new process would increase efficiency while reducing cycle time, waste, and costs. Those are all great objectives for a project, and I was happily capturing them in the charter document. Thankfully the internal customer—a VP for the manufacturing company—was in the room. He allowed the discussion about objectives to go on for a while. Then he stood up and said, "Stop. There's not a single thing you've written down that speaks to why we're here today. Let me make this crystal clear to you. You have one objective and one objective only. Your objective is to shut this plant down as fast as physically possible. That's the objective. If that means we have to move fifty-year-old technology, I expect you to move it."

In this situation, despite the best of intentions, the team made some bad assumptions. They thought the reason behind the project was to improve efficiency and save money. But shutting the facility down as quickly as possible, at whatever cost, was the actual objective. When assumptions are made and not validated, the wrong project may be executed.

Incorrect assumptions can also plague the work breakdown structure and planning process when face-to-face collaboration is replaced by virtual communication. When we develop the WBS, we are all in the same room, which makes it easy to see if a task is missing or duplicated. For example, if Bob is a design engineer, and Karen is a test engineer, they may be in different corners of the room developing their respective task lists with their teams. However, as their work is intertwined, in reality it may be unclear who actually "owns" which task. Since they are in the same room, they can immediately ask the question and agree where it belongs in the WBS. Now compare that to what happens when the WBS is developed virtually. Each person on Bob's team puts together their best guess of the task list and sends it to the other internal team members for feedback. Meanwhile, Karen's team does the same thing within her group. There are two issues here. First, some team members will never get around to reviewing the list, while others will only give it a cursory glance. A robust, collaborative conversation that leads to finding missing tasks and drives clarity does not take place. Second, even if someone does think to question whether a task belongs to Bob's team versus Karen's, they probably don't actually ask the question "out loud" because they're trying to get the "Develop Task List" item checked off their to-do list. Again, the necessary conversation to clarify who actually has responsibility for the activity doesn't take place. So Bob believes Karen is going to do it, while Karen believes Bob is going to do it. Or they both do it, and the task is duplicated. These issues are avoided when we plan face-to-face.

When team members interact in person, they naturally have conversations. And while they may not see eye-to-eye on certain points, they learn to respect each other. They learn to understand why someone in product development thinks differently than someone in marketing. This removes the tendency to see people with different skill sets or in different functional areas as enemies and, as a result, helps foster teamwork.

## FACE-TO-FACE COLLABORATION AIDS PROBLEM SOLVING

When you pull teams together that normally interact via email and instead facilitate face-to-face interaction, problems get solved more quickly and effectively.

In 2016 I worked with an engineering team that was tasked with developing a product based on the voice of the customer research conducted by marketing. In this instance, the marketing team was the client. Following our process my client brought the team together and developed the charter and project plan. The team started with a common assumption: Whatever the customer wants is possible. With that assumption, the team got to work planning the product. They developed a timeline based on including each function marketing had requested. At the end of the session, marketing asked, "How long will that take to create?"

If engineering had included every feature and function marketing wanted, the product would have been ready by December of 2020, a year after marketing had planned its release. Marketing wasn't happy with this result. They wanted a December 2019 release, meaning we had to squeeze a year out of the existing plan. As a team, we started compressing the project to meet the December 2019 deadline. Finally, after doing everything we could think of to hit that deadline, we went back to marketing and said, "The earliest we can get this to you is June of 2020."

But marketing didn't want a June 2020 release. They wanted a December 2019 release. So marketing asked engineering, "What's the hold up?" And engineering said, "The holdup is feature $x$. If we drop that feature, we can get you back to December of 2019."

Marketing asked several follow-up questions and, after some analysis, said, "Okay, we'll do that. Cutting that feature will probably cost us twenty percent of the revenue, which is certainly not insignificant, but we'd rather have eighty percent of something than one hundred percent of nothing."

Was marketing ecstatic about removing that feature? No. Removing it meant they had one less feature that would make their product stand out against competitors and one less feature they could charge for. However, the process of project management involves negotiation. In a perfect world the time, cost, quality levers would be controlled by the project team and have unrestricted movement, but in the real world, there's a constant negotiation of moving those levers in the way that makes sense for the project. With this project it made more sense to forsake a feature than miss the launch date. When done correctly negotiation will lead to a solution that is good enough for the customer and that the

> "Things which matter most must never be at the mercy of things which matter least."
>
> —Johann Wolfgang von Goethe

team can still commit to. What you don't want is a "paper schedule," meaning that the project looks good on paper but will never work in real life.

Without getting everyone in the same room to build relationships and accountability, this agreement could have taken longer or not happened at all. Without having these conversations, marketing might have assumed that engineering couldn't meet its deadline because it simply didn't want to. However, during a face-to-face planning session, marketing will see that engineering is working diligently to meet the deadline with the full set of desired features and understand which specific sequence of activities is holding up the project. At the same time, marketing will be able to clearly articulate which features are nonnegotiable for the project to remain viable. Working together, marketing and engineering will find a solution that solves the problem.

## ACCOUNTABILITY ENCOURAGES SACRIFICE

At the end of each planning session, a compression session is required. The compression session compares the desired target completion date to the current (as scheduled) completion date for the project. Usually, there is a gap between the two, so something needs to change. Either activity precedence relationships, durations, or scope needs to change to close that gap. This is one of my favorite parts of project planning because it further solidifies the team that has already been working for three or more days to plan the project. How? By forcing all the people in the room to look at their activities and make decisions and sacrifices to ensure the project will meet its deadline. It forces them to actively be team players.

When someone in the planning session says, "You know what, I can do task X in two days instead of four," it puts pressure on the rest of the team members to find their own way to help get the project back on track. When one team member sees someone else making a sacrifice, he or she feels obligated to do the same. Not only does the person feel a part of a team, he or she doesn't want to be the only person who isn't making sacrifices for the greater good. The team member also knows that at some point in the project they may need help from others, and they want the assurance that when they need help, someone will return the favor and come to their rescue.

## BUILD ACCOUNTABILITY FOR EACH TASK

Working on large projects requires building accountability between team members and building accountability for each task.

In Chapter 2 I asked whether you had ever experienced the hypothetical situation where several individuals were asked to complete a single task, but no one did. Well, I was referencing something I actually experienced. I had sent an email to several staff members asking them to take care of a task while I was on vacation. When I returned, I learned the task hadn't been done. I was furious! I said, "There were four people on this email. Any one of you could have finished this task. Why didn't it get done?" They all looked around until someone finally said, "Well, we assumed that one of the other people included in the email was doing it." This is an excellent, albeit painful, parable about responsibility.

Unless one person clearly owns a task, you risk running into the "anybody could have, everybody should have, but nobody did" situation. This is why two of our core principles are that only one person can take ownership for a task, and they must be present in the room (this is a welcome respite to those that work in environments where they are afraid to leave the room because, when they do, their name gets assigned to everything). He or she might leverage ten different resources to help do the work, but that one person is the person who makes sure the task gets done.

## THE ROLE OF THE ACTIVITY MANAGER

The Project Success Method uses activity managers to ensure that every task gets done. During the planning session for any project, we create a work breakdown structure, which is a list of all the project activities that we can think of at the moment. *At the moment* is important here because it's rare that even the best teams will catch every single task that must be completed at the very beginning of a project. The activities will not be in any particular order, as sequencing will not have taken place yet. They also won't necessarily have an owner or a duration. It will literally just be a list of activities.

## CENTURY MANUFACTURING COMPANY
### (Work Breakdown Structure)

**MELBOURNE PLANT DEVELOPMENT**
**(Anders)**

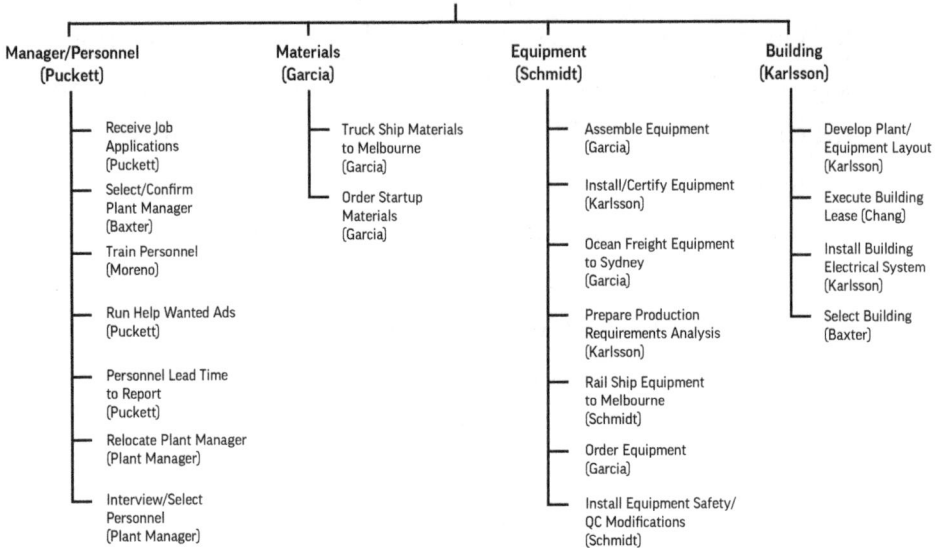

**Manager/Personnel (Puckett)**
- Receive Job Applications (Puckett)
- Select/Confirm Plant Manager (Baxter)
- Train Personnel (Moreno)
- Run Help Wanted Ads (Puckett)
- Personnel Lead Time to Report (Puckett)
- Relocate Plant Manager (Plant Manager)
- Interview/Select Personnel (Plant Manager)

**Materials (Garcia)**
- Truck Ship Materials to Melbourne (Garcia)
- Order Startup Materials (Garcia)

**Equipment (Schmidt)**
- Assemble Equipment (Garcia)
- Install/Certify Equipment (Karlsson)
- Ocean Freight Equipment to Sydney (Garcia)
- Prepare Production Requirements Analysis (Karlsson)
- Rail Ship Equipment to Melbourne (Schmidt)
- Order Equipment (Garcia)
- Install Equipment Safety/QC Modifications (Schmidt)

**Building (Karlsson)**
- Develop Plant/Equipment Layout (Karlsson)
- Execute Building Lease (Chang)
- Install Building Electrical System (Karlsson)
- Select Building (Baxter)

Again, here is an example from the Melbourne Plant Development project in Chapter 1. For that project, we were tasked with establishing a manufacturing and warehousing facility with ten-thousand-square-meters of production, warehouse, and office space; procuring materials for the first month of production; installing ten equipment cells; and hiring thirty employees. Here, each column represents a deliverable. One column includes equipment activities, one includes building activities, one includes materials, and one addresses personnel. Under each column, we list the activities—in no particular order—that have to be completed to finish the project.

Each task has an owner—that is, an activity manager. This means *one person* per activity.

The activity manager agrees to make sure the work gets done. This is the person who looks at the project manager and says, "That's my task. I'll make sure it happens." This doesn't mean they have agreed to do the physical labor themselves, only that they agree to be the single point of contact regarding the activity. The single point of contact concept is very important, as it reduces confusion and adds clarity about who owns the task. In project work, black and white are your friends—gray is your enemy. Anything gray and ambiguous will get used against you in the court of project management. Remember, if you confuse you lose!

## MANAGING RESOURCES

Not only does the activity manager own the task, but he or she also serves as the interface between the team and the resources. Rather than having every resource go to weekly project update meetings, the activity manager attends the meetings and provides updates based on conversations with the resources.

Although the project manager is responsible for the project as a whole, and the activity managers have accepted responsibility for their individual tasks, the project manager is not typically the person who performs the manual labor to complete the tasks (I'll talk more about this in Chapter 6). The resource is the one who actually digs the ditch, writes the code, or designs the widget. The activity manager might have only a single resource available or they may have twenty-five, but he or she takes responsibility for those resources getting their tasks done. In some instances, the activity manager may not have any resources available, in which case they become the de facto resource.

The project manager, in coordination with the activity managers and functional managers, is the one who gets more resources for projects, if needed, and is also the one who works with management to ensure the expectations of those resources are realistic. They accomplish this by escalating the issue(s) through the chain of command.

## BUDGETING RESOURCES

A mistake teams often make during planning is to assume they have unlimited resources. This is a completely incorrect assumption. The fact is, budgets are always limited, and you almost never get all the resources you need. When a schedule is built using this assumption, the team is likely able to meet the requested project deadlines, at least on paper, much to the joy of management. Unfortunately, the schedule is accepted as having been promised by the team and the asterisk of "*assumes unlimited resources" is quickly forgotten. You'll never get the additional resources needed to perform in the now-promised time.

As a project manager, you should never allow the team to plan under this assumption. To effectively plan the project, you have to determine realistic durations based on the number of resources you *currently* have and only change them if and when additional resources are allocated for the project. This protects the team from committing to unrealistic schedules and puts the pressure on management to provide the required resources. Therefore, the project manager should remind the activity managers to think about these questions as they determine their durations for each task:

- What equipment, materials, staff, space, and so on do you need to do this?

- How available are you to work on this?

- What resources can you realistically bring to bear on this?

- Which resources do you not have that you need me to help secure?

Budgeting resources requires looking at the physical resources doing the work and calculating the hours required to get that work done. Once that is done, you can now identify the periods of overload. These are periods of time, typically weeks or months, where the number of hours required to complete the work assigned to a specific resource exceeds the hours that resource has available. Finally, you must resolve these overloads by either increasing resource availability or decreasing the workload during each affected period.

Options for increasing staff resource availability include:

- Use your staffing analysis as the basis for requesting additional personnel.

- Use overtime.

- Use temporary personnel.

- Reschedule discretionary items such as vacation, training, and the like.

Options for decreasing staff resource workload include:

- Reassign project or nonproject work to someone that has availability.

- Contract out the work.

- Use a less labor-intensive approach.

- Delay the start, or extend the duration of, *noncritical* activities to a period where availability exists.

- Cancel or postpone lower priority projects.

Options to avoid, if possible, include:

- Authorized reduction in project scope

- Authorized extension of project duration

Remember, if you do not proactively resolve the overload(s), it will usually be resolved for you by either finishing the project late or hitting the date with "something" (reduced scope and poor quality) that no one is proud of.

## DON'T LET ANYONE HIDE BEHIND ANYTHING

To drive accountability at the activity level, a team member must do three things:

1. Claim ownership of the activity. A team member needs to say, "That's my task—put my name on it." The project manager or functional manager should not assign it—the individual activity manager needs to claim ownership.

2. That same activity manager must now give you the duration for the task. The duration *must* come from that person—no one else, including the associated functional manager.

3. Finally, the person needs to identify the other tasks that must be completed before beginning the task (in other words—the predecessors).

By doing these three things, each person has accepted full responsibility for the task. They now own it!

If project management is done in an ad hoc way, everyone working on the project has plenty of ways to deflect blame. Let's go back to Joe and Cara. Say I'm their project manager, and I send Joe and Cara an email that says, "Here are the three things we need you to get done for project X. Here are the deadlines. Make sure they happen."

That approach gives Cara and Joe three things to hide behind. First, neither of them thinks the activities really belong to them. Cara feels Joe should be doing them, and Joe feels Cara should. Since neither one claims ownership, there is no accountability. Second, Cara and Joe are given durations that are not realistic given the requirements of the other five projects each of them is working on. Consequently, their commitment to hitting those dates is nil. Third, Joe and Cara were not able to identify what information is required from others in order to get the tasks done even though they are in the best position to tell me the order of events. When the tasks don't get done on time, Cara and Joe can legitimately say, "We never agreed that these tasks belonged to us, the durations were wrong, and we couldn't start on the dates you picked because we didn't have the information we needed to get started."

Creating accountability means removing all excuses. It means getting Joe and Cara in the room so *they* can assign *their* names to their activities, determine *their* durations, and explain *what they need* before they can do task X, Y, or Z.

## DON'T UNDERESTIMATE THE PSYCHOLOGY OF EXCLUSION

You should never underestimate the psychology of exclusion. I've worked with many people on many projects, and there's a lot more that goes into excuses than incorrectly setting durations or assigning tasks to someone who isn't in the room.

It's human nature to get upset when we're not included from the get-go in something we're expected to participate in and be held accountable for. While people won't always consciously recognize that they're resisting a duration or activity, subconsciously they're likely irritated that you didn't include them in the planning, and that you didn't think it was worth your time to talk about the task. This exclusion creates a barrier between what the team member is willing to do and your expectations.

Teams using the Project Success Method spend at least three days together planning a project, so they really form a bond. In those short three days, they suffer together, they make hard decisions together, and they sacrifice for each other. At the end of those planning sessions, when the software confirms that the project is going to meet their deadline, they celebrate together. Sometimes to the extreme. They hug, they jump up and down, they shout, and they congratulate each other on a job well done, and I've got the video to prove it. The relationships formed through the trials and tribulations of planning and compression don't dissipate when they go back to their desks. They remain accountable to each other, they respect each other, and they do whatever they need to do to make sure that as a team they succeed.

---

"The things which are most important don't always scream the loudest."

—Bob Hawke

---

# CHAPTER 5 KEY TAKEAWAYS

- Always make people feel like they matter.

- Develop teams that are accountable to each other and to individual tasks.

- Face-to-face, collaborative planning sessions are key to developing accountability among team members.

- Face-to-face collaboration abolishes incorrect assumptions, aids problem solving, and encourages sacrifice.

- Activity managers are responsible for making sure their tasks are completed, but the resources assigned physically perform the work.

- Do not exclude team members during planning. Their inclusion fosters accountability and drives project success.

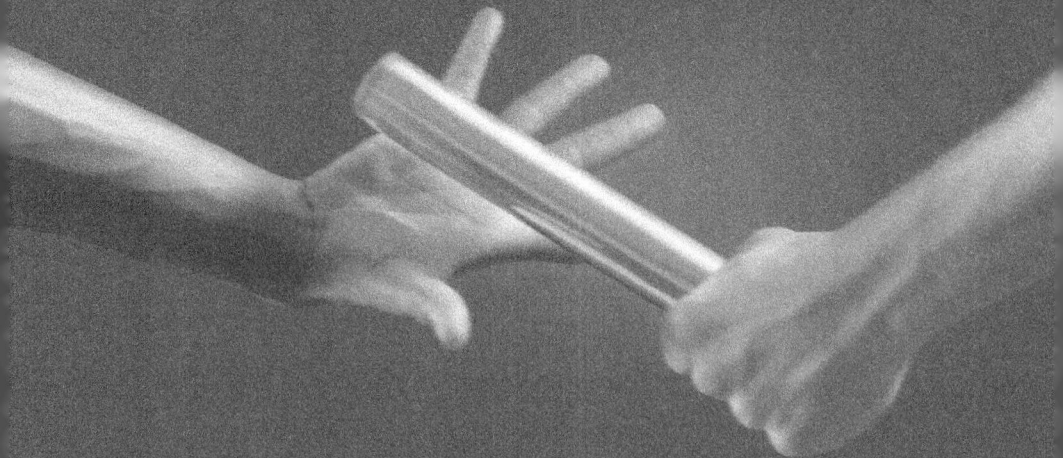

"You don't lead by hitting people over the head. That's assault, not leadership."

—DWIGHT D. EISENHOWER

# CHAPTER 6:

# PLAN FOR THE KNOWN UNKNOWNS, THEN DEAL WITH THE UNKNOWN UNKNOWNS

*PROJECT PLANNING IS* like climbing Mount Kilimanjaro. The easy part is sitting on your couch routing your climb, outlining the things you'll need, and identifying the support team you'll need to complete the ascent. But what happens once you start climbing? Everything changes.

If you are three hours into your climb, and you find the path you've taken is washed out, you're not going to give up on your goal, so you have to find a different route. You have to make a course correction. Maybe you go back to the trailhead and choose a new path to the top. This causes you to lose a few hours, but you'll still get to the top. Or maybe you decide to stay near where the trail has washed out and veer to the right until you meet up with the trail again. Whichever option you choose, your decision is a course correction.

You don't change your goal of getting to the top; you change *the plan* to get there. The same thing happens with projects. You start down one path, realize it's not working, make a course correction, get back on track, and keep going.

Whenever I share this with technical teams, it creates a lot of angst because they feel this burning need to make the exactly perfect decision and build the ideal plan. But with project management, the minute you finish your plan, things begin to change. A task that you didn't think about will come up; you'll learn something new about an activity that means its duration needs to change; you'll learn about a new regulation that will affect the project—the possibilities are endless. Like climbing Mount Kilimanjaro, your project plan isn't static. It's in constant flux, and to deal with these changes, project teams have to make countless course corrections. And that's OK because *control sessions* allow us to make those corrections every week or two. At the end of each control session, the plan is valid and accurate again.

> "Give someone responsibility and they will do their best. Make them accountable and they will do even better."
>
> —Simon Sinek

This means your initial plan doesn't have to be perfect. You just have to be willing to put the work in with the team every week or two to bring the plan up to date and take the necessary actions to get it back on track. There will be times when you go down a path that ends up not working, forcing you to reevaluate your goals. Should we kill the project (give up on our goal of reaching the peak of Kilimanjaro) or choose a different path to reach the top? There are many things that can force you off your original, planned path but a large majority of them fall into two categories—known unknowns and unknown unknowns. Fortunately, our initial project plan will allow us to address both and keep us out of the ditch!

## WHAT ARE KNOWN UNKNOWNS?

Known unknowns are the things you know will happen during a project; you just don't know when or how much they will affect the project. Someone will get sick; that's known. But you don't know who it will be, when they'll get sick, or how long they'll be out. That's the unknown. Someone else will have to go to a training event they weren't aware of while planning their activities, and someone else will be late on an activity. These are all known events, but you won't know when the training will happen, or who it will happen to, or which team member will be late on which activities. This group can be further subdivided into the parts you can address while building your plan, like reworking and debugging, and the parts that you have to wait to address when the monster raises its ugly head, such as illness.

I once worked on a project with a brilliant engineer who had great technical skills but had a huge blind spot for project management. This client used a term called "percent new content." Percent new content means you're introducing something completely new to an existing design. This has broad impact because when you change one part of a design, dozens of other things can be impacted. The higher the percentage of new content, the riskier the project. Because we know this, between each phase of design, we plan time for debugging and reworking. We know something won't work (the known), we just don't know which part of the design won't work or exactly how long it will take to fix (the unknown). I don't know which module is going to break or which part is going to fail, but I know for a fact that in a complex project or one that has a higher percentage of new content something will fail. I need to build time into the schedule to fix it. That's a known unknown. Because we've worked on so many projects, we can account for this known unknown in the schedule by using our own experience. If past projects of similar complexity (percent new content) required six weeks of debugging, we can use six weeks as our placeholder.

This engineer, who was also serving as the project manager on that project, wasn't happy when I added time for debugging and reworking after each iteration of design. He said that I was planning for failure, and that I should plan for success instead—get it right the first time. If I had followed his advice and removed the debugging and reworking time from the schedule, his team would have to have been 100 percent right every single time for the project to stay on schedule—which is clearly impossible, regardless of how good they are.

Project managers should always consider known unknowns and address them in their project plans so they can build realistic schedules that the team actually believes in and that enable them to deliver high-quality projects on time. Build time in your plans for debug, rework, approvals, permits, and so on by including them as activities even if you're unsure of the duration. Use your best guess as a placeholder since you can always make it more accurate later when you have better knowledge.

## KNOWN UNKNOWNS AND INTERNATIONAL SPORTING EVENTS

Tens of thousands of activities must be completed for international sporting events such as the Olympic Games or the FIFA World Cup to happen. One known unknown that can really hold up the process is approvals, especially logo approvals.

Olympic logo approval, for example, requires significant communication with the International Olympic Committee (IOC). The process starts when the IOC creates the logo for that specific Olympic Games. After the logo is created, major sponsors take the logo and add their own logo to it. The new logo, which integrates the IOC logo and the sponsor's logo, is called a composite logo. The sponsor sends the composite logo to the IOC for approval. The initial composite logo design is rarely approved, necessitating many rounds of design modifications and resubmissions before acceptance is achieved. Consequently, composite logo approval is one of several long, drawn-out processes in planning an international sporting event. It's also a very challenging known unknown.

If a sponsor can't get their logo approved or approval takes too long, they can't finish other activities like incorporating the composite logo into the final uniform designs, which, by the way, also must be submitted for approval. This is problematic because of the long lead times on uniform procurement to obtain optimal pricing. Anyone working on major international sporting event planning knows how slow logo approvals can be. It's a known unknown that has to be planned for, or you risk not being ready in time for the event.

## WHAT ARE UNKNOWN UNKNOWNS?

Unknown unknowns are the crazy things that happen that you could never in a million years plan for. Things like the tsunami that destroyed Japan's Fukushima Daiichi Nuclear Power Plant. No one knew that tsunami was coming, until it was too late. That is an unknown unknown. Thankfully, most projects don't encounter such devastating unknown unknowns; however, unknown unknowns come in all shapes and sizes and need to be planned for. Here's an extreme example I dealt with several years ago.

I worked with a major manufacturer of agricultural equipment on a project to design and bring to production a new agriculture tractor concept. It was a huge undertaking because it was a complete redesign of an existing agriculture tractor. For example, the new tractor was designed to run on tracks rather than four wheels.

During the prove design phase, the initial design is completed, special unique parts are produced, and a prove design tractor (prototype) is built and tested. Learnings from that testing inform the next phase of design. For this tractor project, one of the many prototype components was a one-of-a-kind transmission. On the way to deliver that transmission to the assembly facility, the truck carrying it jackknifed and destroyed the transmission it was hauling. This catastrophe was going to add months to our project plan. We had no idea that was going to happen. It's never happened before on any project I've worked on, and it's never happened since. This is what we call an unknown unknown.

## HOW DO YOU MANAGE KNOWN UNKNOWNS AND UNKNOWN UNKNOWNS?

Plan for known unknowns by building time into your schedule to address these risk factors. If you're building a product, you know you need time for debugging and reworking. If you're working on a project that requires numerous supervisory approvals, you know those will take time. Therefore, build time for rework and multiple iterations of approval into the schedule.

A common known unknown that will need to be addressed in every project is illness. We know one of our team members is going to get sick during the project, but we have no idea who, when, or for how long. So how do you account for that up front during planning? Some people like to add a buffer as a safety net, either by adding extra time to each of their activity durations or by having one big buffer that the project manager owns and parcels out as needed during the project. I strongly disagree with this approach for two reasons. First, let's observe the impact of arbitrarily inflating all of your activities by only a seemingly small number like two days. If your critical path has thirty activities—and some will have many, many more—you just added sixty working days, which is three calendar months, to your schedule. Now, everybody looks at the timeline and knows something's not right. They know that you are sandbagging and no longer trust the schedule—or you. Second, I think the buffer that the project manager parcels out probably works—once. It's hard to beat human nature, and people are smart. Let's say that I'm a team member on a project where you are the project manager. I have an activity that is running late, and it's on the critical path. I am feeling really anxious because there is simply no way that I'm going to be able to complete the task on time, and I'm going to be the reason the project finishes late. But then I remember. "Wait a minute. I've worked with Amber before, and she's a great project manager. She's got my back! She has this twenty-day buffer that she uses for situations like this. I only need three days! Yes!" The problem is that ten different people on the team are having that same exact thought, so now Amber's buffer needs to be thirty days. So this is a technique that might work once or twice, but then people realize that the "magical buffer" exists and build it into their assumptions or take the pressure off themselves to finish on time because they have a safety net.

So how should it be handled instead? You can't handle this during planning, but you can use your plan to address the illness when it comes up. Once we learn that Kimberly is sick, we identify the activities belonging to her that are scheduled to take place over the window of time she expects to be out. We then look at the amount of flexibility each of these tasks contains. We delay those tasks that have enough flexibility that they can start when she returns from her illness. The activities that do not have enough flexibility—meaning they would delay the project if they were delayed—need to be assigned to someone else. While we couldn't plan for the illness in advance, despite knowing it would occur, we use our plan to address the illness when it actually happens.

Managing the unknown unknowns requires flexibility because there's no way to plan for them upfront. Since you can't just abandon your plan when an unknown unknown happens, be prepared to ask, "What can I do now?"

---

## BE FLEXIBLE

When you hit an unknown, known or otherwise, you may have to go backward ten steps to go forward twenty. Whatever you end up doing, you'll need the cooperation of your team to do it. This requires flexibility and people skills. To do this, you have to plan for and be ready to address the known unknowns and the unknown unknowns that could otherwise derail your project. There will be times when you go down a path that ends up not working. You'll have to abandon that path and find a different way to achieve your goal of getting the project done to the customer's satisfaction. When you're six hours into climbing Mount

Kilimanjaro and encounter a washed-out trail, you may be forced to travel back down the mountain for three hours in order to switch to a different trail that is now your best chance for a successful ascent. That is clearly frustrating because you feel like you have wasted six hours. You'll encounter these same frustrations when a course correction is required in your project. The team has invested weeks or months of their time in following a certain path and will feel like it was all wasted when a different path is required to achieve a successful project.

---

When the tractor trailer delivering the transmission jackknifed, we took two approaches. One team went to the crash site, swept up the parts, and returned to the lab to see if they could somehow save the transmission. We didn't know whether it was possible to repair what remained or whether the transmission would work in the event that it was salvaged. With that in mind, we had a second team research whether there was a transmission on the market that was similar enough to the one that had been destroyed that it could be modified and used for our purpose. Unfortunately, neither approach was successful.

Having explored those two options, we went to management and said, "As you know, the prove design transmission was destroyed, so we need to create a new one. It's going to take a few months for that to happen. Therefore, we'd like permission to change the deadline."

Unfortunately, management said no. They'd already talked about the transmission at numerous farm shows and wanted it ready by the current deadline. We went back and beat our heads against the wall until someone said, "I have an idea for how we could hit the deadline without breaking the laws of physics, but it's risky. We could hit the current deadline if we drop one iteration of design—go from a four-phase process to a three-phase process."

We looked at each phase and the associated risks of dropping it. Based on our analysis, we were able to recommend which iteration was the best to alleviate. We presented our recommendation to management and explained the associated risks they would need to agree to take on. Ultimately, management approved our recommendation, and we got the project back on track. That's how you handle unknown unknowns. You pause, you look at your plan, including the bad news from the unknown unknowns, and as a team answer the question "What can we do to get this thing back on track?"

## GET COMMITMENT FROM THE TEAM MEMBER, NOT THEIR MANAGER

The fact of the matter is that the duration needs to come from, and make sense to, *the person who will carry out the task*. Most people who have experience working in project management as team members aren't used to this approach. They're used to their project manager or functional manager setting the durations without any input from them. This never works.

My least favorite expression in project management is "make it happen." The literal translation of this is that a miracle will occur, and everything will work out. Unfortunately, a miracle is not going to occur, and *everybody knows it*. You have to set durations that make sense so that "it" does happen.

Too often, managers give their subordinates durations that are unrealistic. This happens because the employee's work always looks a lot easier to somebody who's not physically doing it, or maybe the manager is an expert at the task and assumes it will be just as easy for the employee. This is particularly true as you move up the chain of command, and your boss's boss thinks your work looks *really* simple. Out of that come two biases. One, they will assume that because your work looks simple, you won't need much time to do it. Two, that person will think about your job in the context of the one task needed for the project. They think, "Task X isn't very complicated, so it shouldn't take him more than three days to finish it."

What the manager doesn't consider, or more likely isn't aware of, is that Jim is also working on six other tasks in parallel, and in a week he'll be going to a training event that will pull him off all projects for three days (a known unknown that has now become a known known). In reality it's going to take Jim three weeks to find the three days he will need to get that task done. Not three days, three weeks. So if Jim and his boss don't have a conversation about the duration of the task and what's realistic, and Jim's boss instead assigns him a duration, Jim likely won't get it done by the mandated deadline and has absolutely *no* buy-in. We have created another paper schedule that looks good on paper but isn't going to happen in real life.

I don't think functional or project managers do this on purpose. I don't think they want to see the project fail, but with typical project management, they assign durations rather than sitting down with their team and setting realistic ones. Or

During our planning process, we focus on the team members and ask them to set realistic durations that they can commit to.

they back-schedule and think, "Well, they only have three days to get this done," believing that means the team member has no option but to get the activity done in that span of time.

During our planning process, we focus on the team members and ask them to set realistic durations that they can commit to. If Jane is the activity manager, and she wants ten working days to complete the task, but her manager, Bridgette, thinks she only needs two working days, we need to resolve this conflict. We'll start with asking Jane why she needs ten days to complete the task. This is Jane's opportunity to explain that "it's ten days because I've got four other projects I am working on in parallel with this one, and I need to conduct some research regarding the issues prior to tackling this task, plus I am in training for two days during that period. It's not like I'm going to devote one hundred percent of my time to this one task for ten days."

Next, we ask Bridgette how she came up with two days. Bridgette replies, "OK, I wasn't aware that Jane was working on four additional projects. I knew she had more than one, but I wasn't aware it was four. Knowing that, I don't think two days is realistic, but I still don't think it's ten. What Jane doesn't know is that some of this work was already completed before she came onboard. We already developed a lot of this intellectual property on a previous project. If she uses that as her starting point, she definitely won't need ten days—probably closer to five days."

So we have this conversation, and at the end we look at Jane and say, "Jane, what do you want for your duration?"

Jane says, "That's great news about the previously developed intellectual property. With that new information, I think I'd be comfortable dropping the duration to seven days … at least for now. I'll take a look at what's available and let you know if I want to drop the duration further. I can't commit to five days at this time because I haven't seen the previous work that was done, but I think seven is doable."

As a result, we get a compromise on a duration that will be much more realistic than anything Bridgette would have set had the conversation not happened. What we will never do is write down a duration that has been set by Bridgette for a task that Jane has ownership of as the activity manager. If we can't get a compromise, we'll either assign Bridgette as the owner/activity manager along with her duration of two days, or we'll keep Jane as the activity manager and write down the duration of ten days. It's the only way to build accountability. Otherwise, Jane walks out of the room having been allotted two days for the task, thinking to herself, "Well, they only gave me two days, but it's not going to happen. It's going to take me two weeks, so I'm being set up for failure. Why won't they listen to me?" You cannot get trust or accountability from team members if you set durations for them.

Facilitating this conversation and ultimately protecting the activity manager's duration requires fortitude on the part of the project manager. An added benefit is Jane now truly understands that you have her back, and she recognizes you are willing to work with her as a partner on the project. I suspect your project just became Jane's favorite one, and she'll be more likely to work with you to resolve an issue if things go sideways.

## BE TRULY WILLING TO CHANGE DURATIONS

Going into a project, we know that some durations will change. The known unknowns and unknown unknowns guarantee this. Often during a planning session, when asked for a duration, the team member will respond, "I can't tell you how long it takes until you tell me when it starts." Of course, this makes sense from that person's perspective. After all, a duration for an activity that starts next week (when the team member is fully committed to other work) will be different from the duration for a task that starts six months from now, when two of their current projects have closed out. In order to answer the question, we would need to know when each preceding activity started and finished. This is quite difficult to do during the initial planning because each preceding activity manager is saying the same thing: "Tell me when it starts, and I'll tell you how long it takes." Now we have a classic chicken and egg scenario. But this can be resolved if the project manager is willing to let team members change durations. *A fundamental ground rule of inclusive project management is to allow for duration changes when better information allows for improved estimates.*

People with punitive experience in project management won't believe the project manager is going to allow them to change the duration later. They think, "Yeah, that sounds great, but my seventeen years of working at ACME Corporations say different. What really happens is whatever duration I give them today is cast in stone and used to club me over the head with for the rest of the project. I'm never actually allowed to change it."

Say Vivek is of this mindset. He doesn't trust his project manager to be open to changing the duration later. He thinks, "That task would probably take me about six hours if I focused on it exclusively." He then thinks, "I'm not sure right now exactly when this task will show up on my to-do list, but in a typical five-day work week, I should be able to find six hours to complete the task." Since Vivek doesn't believe he can change it later, what duration does he tell the project manager? Five days? Probably not—he builds in a safety net and says ten days. Now we have ten days in the schedule for a task Vivek really only felt he needed five days for. How often do you think Vivek finishes his task in five days? Never! Durations become self-fulfilling prophecies.

We are much better served by requiring realistic durations that can be changed later as one gets smarter about the task than by having team members inflate durations to feel safe.

Alternatively, team members who know their project manager will follow through and let them adjust their durations don't do this. They don't add the safety net because they don't need it. They remember the last project they were on with this same project manager, when they lost three days because they were called to jury duty. They didn't feel any pain. Rather than use the delay as a reason to beat them over the head or, worse, still hold them accountable for the original finish date, they were able to extend the duration of their task by three days. It was OK. It was acceptable.

Here's another example of why duration changes must be allowed. Let's say we have an activity that takes place outdoors, where it's subject to the weather. When you ask Rosa for the duration on this task, even if she does believe you'll let her change it later, she's probably going to struggle coming up with a duration. She's going to say, "This task is dependent on the weather. I can't work on it when it rains, and since I can't predict the weather, how can I possibly give you the duration?"

The smart project manager will respond, "Let's build in time for rain to make the duration realistic and as risk mitigation. Further, I realize the rain patterns are different in the summer than the winter, and since we won't know exactly when this task is going to be scheduled until we finish the planning session, let's assume annual rainfall probability for now."

Rosa says, "OK, where this task takes place, the chance of rain is about twenty percent, so we can expect to lose approximately one day a week to rain." Her initial proposed duration, thinking about the effort (number of actual hours) needed, which she then adjusted for her availability without the rain risk, was twenty days—so she needs twenty dry days. Assuming five-day work weeks, she needs four dry weeks. Since we're anticipating a 20 percent rainfall impact, she'll lose four days to rain during those four weeks. Therefore, the duration she plans for is twenty-four days (the initial twenty days plus the four-day risk mitigation for rain).

Furthermore, once the project planning is completed and she has a better idea of *when* the task is expected to take place, she can adjust the duration in anticipation of more or less rain, depending on the season.

The best way to effectively determine durations is to have activity managers set their own durations and for the project manager to understand and accept that durations will change. Get everyone in a room together and plan the project collaboratively. Show your team that project management isn't building a static plan that is never allowed to change or pushing you to complete each and every one of your tasks exactly as planned, but is instead building a plan together that you all believe in and have ownership of. Planning, including duration estimates, is a discussion of what can and cannot be done *realistically*. The planning session provides an early opportunity for setting the tone of everyone making realistic, intelligent decisions in a collaborative way.

---

## BREAKOUT: WORKING WITH CREATIVES

Creatives don't like being boxed in. They are often deadline-averse because they don't feel one can put a timeline on creativity, but their activities are also often on the critical path. Giving creatives the space they need to create while also keeping the critical path on schedule is a balancing act that starts with a single conversation.

During this conversation, I always explain that I don't want to disrupt their process. I acknowledge that yes, we are asking them to follow a structure, but I emphasize that the structure isn't rigid. They can change their durations when needed (again, flexibility).

Then, as with other team members, we'll check in with them along the way to see how things are going. Usually, when they understand and believe that they can adjust their durations, they feel more in control of the process and are a lot easier to work with.

Sometimes people surprise you. I remember working with a concept artist on a project at Caterpillar. His job was to draw the conceptual visualization of the product. Concept artists are clearly artistic folks so I expected some significant pushback when I asked him for a duration on one of his tasks. After all I'd heard, "You can't time box creativity" from many people in the past. Instead, he was very forthcoming with an answer. I mentioned my surprise, and he said, "I recognize the need for a finish date. Otherwise, I'll keep trying to make it better, and it will never actually be done."

A structural approach isn't necessarily a bad thing. A rigid, inflexible structure is.

## SHIFT THE WORRY CURVE

Never assume that giving someone a deadline will put enough pressure on them to get it done. That almost never works. In fact, it just fuels the first phase of the worry curve—uninformed optimism. When Julie gets a deadline assigned to her that she finds arbitrary because she wasn't allowed to participate in setting it, isn't really clear about what the task entails, and is already working on a number of other projects, she'll assume she'll be able to get it done and therefore not worry about it until the last minute, when panic sets in.

When project managers are flexible, when they allow team members to set their own durations and guarantee that durations can be changed in the event of a known unknown or an unknown unknown, those team members become accountable. When that happens, the worry curve shifts.

Don't forget that because we work in a matrix, the only chance of success the project manager has is for all team members to feel obligated and committed to their tasks. Team members who hold themselves accountable for the durations they set and trust their project manager will allow changes are much more likely to meet project deadlines.

## HOW TO RESPOND TO CHANGING DURATIONS

When a team member needs to change the duration of their task, *never* respond negatively.

I've heard confrontational project managers say things like, "You're joking, right? How could you let this happen? You just screwed up the whole schedule. You need to go fix it." Even if they aren't as forceful as this particular project manager, many project managers say the same thing in a slightly less offensive way.

This approach isn't helpful for two reasons. One, the project manager loses any trust they may have had with that team member, which reinforces their view of project management as punitive—not helpful. Two, if the team member could have fixed the issue, he or she would have. No one wants to walk into a room and announce they're the reason a project is now going to be three weeks late.

Our process isn't looking to assign blame. It's looking to maintain a real schedule in the real world while using accountability and collaboration to keep the project on track when bad news comes.

## HOW TO USE RELATIONSHIPS TO COMPENSATE FOR SLIPPAGE

So, what happens when activity durations get extended? It depends. Most of the activities in your project plan will not be on the critical path, so if they are a little late, it won't affect the project completion date. However, if the delayed activity is on the critical path, the project will be delayed. We call that delay slippage. We use control meetings to account for and reduce slippage, so projects stay on schedule. When a team member has to change durations, take that bad news along with the rest of the team's updated information, update the schedule, and identify and remove any slippage.

When we go through this exercise with clients, we project the critical path up on the screen and then figure out, as a team, how to eliminate the slippage. This is where the relationships you've built with your team are extremely important. A team that is accountable and trusts their project manager will do whatever is possible individually to get the project back on track, even if the slippage isn't technically a particular person's fault.

If the team's attitude is, "Hey, man, I didn't break it. I'm not going to fix it," then a project will likely never be completed successfully. The attitude should be "How are *we (the team)* going to get the slippage back?" The attitude team members take toward slippage largely depends on the relationship they have with their teammates, including the project manager. In any project, there will be times when you're asked to fix a problem you did not cause. That's why the collaboration piece is so important. We built the plan as a team, and as a team we compress it back.

Effective project managers are proactive about how they and their team are going to fix a delayed project, as opposed to being negative and reactive about how the slippage happened. Good project managers proactively remind their team about the process, and that team members have to take into account their availability when they set durations, understanding that they're not working on that one task 100 percent of the time. Project managers should remind their teams not to be optimistic or pessimistic but instead plan for what's most likely going to happen, secure in the knowledge they can change that duration later on.

Over time, team members that are led by strong, collaborative, inclusive project managers become more and more accountable to each other. In fact, they almost get competitive about making up for slippage when a project is delayed. If Susan figures out a way to get her task completed two days earlier than planned (by adding resources, resequencing other tasks, or by doing things in parallel) to help make up for a project's eight days of slippage, Jeff might try to save three. You get the sense that the team is almost competing for who can be the biggest hero. Such behavior comes from the obligation, commitment, and accountability that have been fostered by the project manager following the Project Success Method.

# CHAPTER 6 KEY TAKEAWAYS

- Every project will encounter known unknowns, such as debug, rework, and approvals, as well as unknown unknowns, such as natural disasters or accidents. You must plan for the known unknowns that you can identify and use your plan and the team to address the other issues as they arise.

- Managing the unknowns requires flexibility.

- Accept durations that make sense to the person who will carry out the task, the activity manager.

- Set the expectation that durations can be changed later.

- Help your team members shift their worry curve by letting them set their own durations.

- Never respond negatively when someone needs to change a duration. Work with them in a proactive, not reactive, way.

- People and the relationships you've developed with them are the tools that will help account for slippage.

---

"Responsibility equals accountability equals ownership. And a sense of ownership is the most powerful weapon a team or organization can have."

–Pat Summitt

---

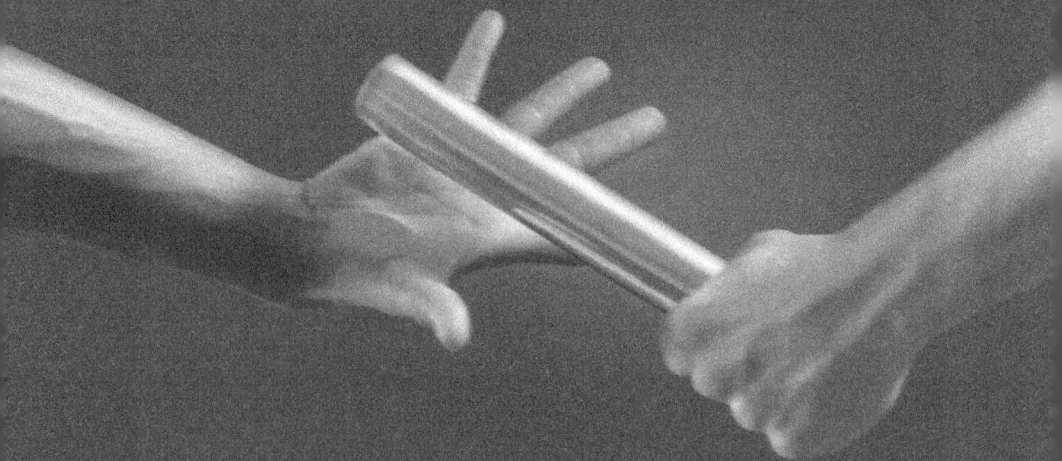

"The future depends on what we do in the present."

—GANDHI

# BE REALISTIC WITH YOUR PROJECT AND YOUR TEAM

*ABOUT TEN YEARS AGO,* I did a project for a major cable network called the High Definition (HD) project. They wanted to have all their New York programming available in HD in time for November midterm election coverage. This was a massive undertaking of equipment procurement, process development, and design, along with the associated installation and testing—all without disrupting regular programming. We started planning in March and wrote an October due date in our charter as our target. However, after three days of planning, we realized that we could not meet the customer's expectations. No matter how hard the team tried, we simply could not meet the deadline the customer wanted given the parameters of the project. Initially, the team tried to meet the requirements by making adjustments on two of the three dimensions of project performance— time and cost—while protecting the quality (project scope) dimension (which is very typical for compression). Unfortunately, this approach was unsuccessful in this case.

We went back to the customer with the project plan that showed them why we couldn't hit our deadline, and they agreed to change the delivery date. They weren't thrilled about the change, of course, but customers are much happier if you tell them during week one that whatever they're hoping for can't be done than if you get three weeks away from delivery and say, "Oh, by the way, we're going to be nine weeks late."

Customers always have targets in terms of scope and timing. During the planning and control processes, it's up to the project manager to help negotiate reducing scope if the project can't be finished on time. The project manager's job is to deliver the project on time and on budget and with all the scope initially agreed to. A project manager who can't manage scope shouldn't be in that role. This includes the ability to say no to internal customers; otherwise, you end up with schedules nobody on the team believes can actually be met. I realize this is easier said than done, but what's the alternative? Promise to deliver everything and then deliver late or with poor quality? Which scenario would you rather live in, the one where you and your team know the schedule is unrealistic, and there is no chance of hitting the deadline or the one where you say no to the customer up front and then negotiate something you can actually deliver? In the first scenario, you spend the entire project with your stomach tied up in knots, praying for a miracle to occur but fully expecting the hammer to drop when someone in senior management finally realizes you aren't going to deliver. Every day you show up at work wondering, "Is this the day they find out?" Alternatively, you say no to unrealistic deadlines at the beginning of the project and negotiate a mix of time/cost and quality that your team can actually deliver. Of course, the stress is higher in the beginning, but life, overall, is much calmer and more relaxed. Plus, your team loves you because you fought for them, unlike almost every other project manager they've ever worked with. And truthfully senior management isn't stupid—they'd rather know you'll push back in the beginning but ultimately deliver than put their trust in a project manager who says "no problem" but then fails.

Allow me to take some liberty with Ben Franklin's famous quote: the bitterness of poor quality remains long after the sweetness of early promises are forgotten.

## DO YOUR JOB, NOT EVERYONE ELSE'S

Some people don't like being a project manager and prefer to avoid it. They recognize that they would rather do their technical job than manage people, and that's great, as long as they don't allow themselves to be forced into the project manager role.

When we plan projects, we place sticky notes on a conference room wall as we develop the project plan. Each sticky note includes the activity description, the activity manager, and the duration for a single task. They are then placed in the order/sequence they will be performed. The result is a network diagram: a visual representation or model for our project (see previous photo in chapter 2).

Many project managers become project managers by promotion whether they want to or not. They have really great technical skills, so they get tagged to be the next project manager, but the reality is that it's not their strength. Their strength is technical detail. They prefer being in a cubicle by themselves rather than managing the project and interacting with the team members. This personality type shouldn't be a project manager. A project manager needs to understand and accept that their job is to manage the project and all it entails, rather than working on their favorite activities within the project. If they don't understand this, they keep taking on more of the work they enjoy, or forcing their expertise on those actually assigned to the tasks, and less of the project manager's time is devoted to actually managing the project—a recipe for disaster.

## RECOGNIZE AND CONTROL PROJECT BURNOUT

You may recall from Chapter 4 my unpleasant experience with the "Bamboo Shaft" professor who, on the first day of class, announced that most students would fail. I remember thinking, "This is crazy," so I dropped the class. I took the class the following quarter with a different professor and, thankfully, passed it. There's simply no way I can work for a boss (or professor) who will give me something he knows I can't do but will hold me accountable for it anyway. That sends a bad message. You cannot have expectations that you know are unrealistic. This always leads to paper schedules, mistrust, evasion, and, eventually, burnout.

## WHAT IS BURNOUT?

According to the Mayo Clinic, job burnout is "a special type of work-related stress—a state of physical or emotional exhaustion that also involves a sense of reduced accomplishment and loss of personal identity."[8] Burnout happens when an individual team member is doing too much. This is often the result of companies starting as many projects as possible. Why? They want to make money. As a result, projects are launched without the appropriate resources to support

---

8   "Job burnout: How to spot it and take action," Mayo Clinic, November 21, 2018, https://www.mayoclinic.org/healthy-lifestyle/adult-health/in-depth/burnout/art-20046642.

them. This puts too much work on each team member's plate and invites serious cases of burnout.

Again referencing the Mayo Clinic, job burnout can result from various factors, including:

- Lack of control

- Unclear job expectations

- Dysfunctional workplace dynamics

- Extremes of activity

- Lack of social support

- Work-life imbalance

The good news is that every one of these can be alleviated by following the Project Success Method process and leveraging the techniques laid out in this book!

I can't tell you how many times a team member has said, "Everyone knows we won't hit that deadline. Why won't the boss change it?" In my experience, people leading companies are generally very smart. They're in the position they're in for a reason. I think bosses sometimes put artificial deadlines out there so that their employees will keep their noses to the grindstone. Think about it. If you're on a project that has a very, very aggressive deadline, but then the deadline is moved to something more realistic, what is your natural reaction? To breathe a sigh of relief and take your foot off the gas. Well, you didn't have time for that; now you're late again! Having said that, we never endorse artificial deadlines. We prefer to work with realistic deadlines. They can be aggressive but not so much so that they can only be accomplished by inventing the flux capacitor, putting it in a DeLorean, and going back in time in order to start the project earlier. Working on projects with impossible deadlines definitely contributes to burnout.

It's very rare for someone to come straight out and tell you they're burned out, but burnout is easy to spot. Team members who are burned out stop attending meetings, avoid their project manager, stop taking their project manager's phone calls, and stop returning emails. If you're lucky enough to catch them in a hallway and have a conversation, they tend to be combative and/or evasive. They also give verbal cues, becoming very negative in their outlook about the project. They may give one-word answers to questions or some other response that indicates they no longer care about the work. It's so depressing for them, they don't want to think about the project and resent being forced to.

## WHAT DAMAGE DOES BURNOUT CAUSE?

It is estimated that job stress costs US businesses between $150 billion and $300 billion annually, based on sick time, long-term disability, and excessive job turnover.[9] From a project perspective, at least three negative impacts come to mind when I think of team member burnout. One, project quality suffers. Under extreme and often unrealistic pressure to get tasks done, people produce poorer quality work. Even if the team member wants to produce good work, when overworked or given unrealistic expectations, he or she begins to take shortcuts. The mentality becomes "That's close enough. It'll have to do. I don't have the time to make it right."

Two, you lose team members. When someone is working eighty hours a week yet knows that still isn't enough to successfully produce a quality product, the team member will get frustrated. He or she

---

9    Steve Nguyen, PHD, "The True Financial Cost of Job Stress," Workplace Psychology, January 9, 2011, https://workplacepsychology. net/2011/01/09/the-true-financial-cost-of-job-stress/.

realizes that not only is it impossible to get everything done, but the completed work will not meet the standard they have set for themselves. When someone overworks to produce inadequate results, he or she often gives up and finds somewhere else to work. As a result, you lose a really good team member. Ironically, I've never seen the cost of losing a team member counted against a project cost, but it should be. Think about the cost associated with driving three team members out of a company. To replace them, you have to pay to recruit, hire, onboard, train, and get the new hires up to speed on a project. That's not cheap. In my mind, if you cause three people to quit, that loss should be attributed to your project cost.

Three, safety problems are more likely. After a few eighty-hour weeks, people get tired. Consequently, they are more prone to make mistakes. In certain work environments, mistakes can lead to severe injury or even death.

## HOW DO YOU PREVENT BURNOUT?

There are two ways to prevent burnout. The first one is for someone in upper management to prioritize projects—particularly in an environment where you have more projects than people on staff to complete them. Most of us work in a multiproject environment, in which all projects are deemed top priority. As I mentioned in Chapter 2, I strongly believe that if everything is top priority, nothing really is; they are all the same priority. Someone needs to be in charge of deciding what the return on investment is to the company for completing project A versus project B. If the decision is to go with project A, A gets priority for the resources.

The second way to prevent burnout is for the project manager to pay close enough attention to his or her team to quickly recognize when a team member has too much work. As soon as the project manager sees this, a visit to management is needed, to say, "There's no way Colleen is going to get all of this work done. We need additional resources." Of course, to make this argument successfully, we need data to support our assertion. The Project Success Method to the rescue!

In a typical corporate environment, there are many projects in flight at any one time. Consequently, the Project Success Method understands that in any given week almost every team member will have more tasks assigned than can be done in that period. This is why understanding the critical path is so important. Say a project has one thousand tasks. Of those tasks, maybe 10 percent, or one hundred tasks, will be on the critical path. The other nine hundred aren't critical, meaning that even if they're finished late, the project will still meet the deadline. So if Colleen looks at her activities for the week and sees that she needs to get thirty done, but only six of them are critical path items, she can focus on those six. She can use any time she has left to focus on the noncritical path items that are closest to becoming critical.

Using the Project Success Method, we would look at each of the tasks Colleen was responsible for within a, say, two-week window of time. First, we'd look at the tasks that are on the critical path. Remember, critical path tasks have to be done, or they will delay the project. For example: Colleen has six tasks for three different projects on the critical path. She knows that she will not be able to get all six done, so she has a conversation with the project manager. Based on that conversation, the project manager approaches Colleen's functional manager to see if some of the tasks can be reassigned to someone that has availability. If that is not possible, the project manager must go to senior management to obtain agreement on which of the projects is the most important and which ones can be delayed. A project manager who isn't paying attention to team members and their workloads and actively working to resolve the periods of overload will end up with burned-out team members. This is obviously bad for team members, but it's also detrimental for the projects and the company, as it ultimately results in failed projects.

For instance, an HR director for a Fortune 50 company called me and said that he was being set up for failure and needed my help. He told me that he had been tasked with twelve projects for the next fiscal year, but he didn't believe he could complete them all with his existing staff. We helped him plan all twelve projects and then resource-load those projects with the resources he was most worried might be overloaded. He then prioritized all twelve projects from most important ("could lose my job") to least important ("if I have time left over"). We then created resource histograms for each resource assigned to his highest priority project and checked to ensure none was overloaded.

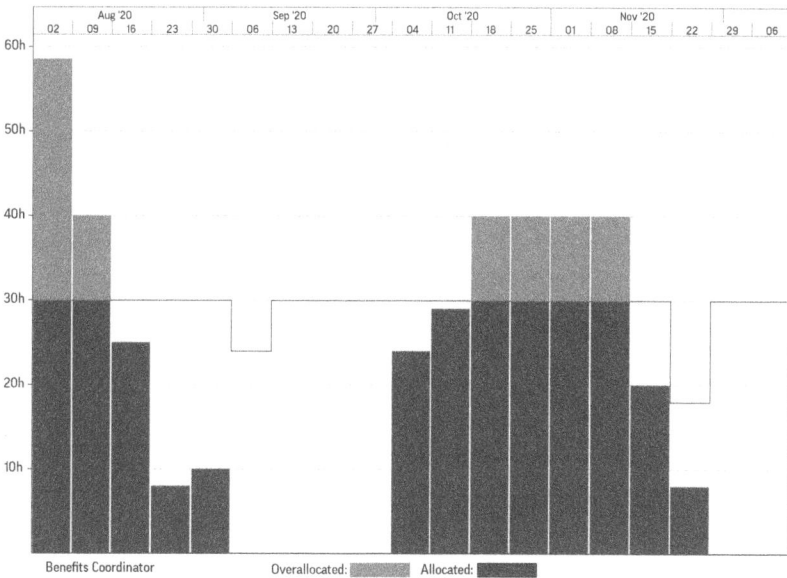

*Resource Histogram: Columns indicate work assigned (in hours) to Colleen each week. The horizontal line shows her availability.*

We continued to check the histograms for overloads as we added additional projects to the "pile." Eventually, we were at seven projects on the pile and everyone was at capacity, except for three, who were overloaded. I'd love to be able to tell you that he only had to get seven projects done that year, and he got the additional resources needed, but my stories are true stories, and that's not what happened. His boss, the VP of HR, asked, "How many hours a week are you working your team?" The director said, "Forty," to which the VP replied, "Then make it fifty." By increasing the availability from forty to fifty hours per week, we were able to get two more projects on the pile. But at the end of the day, the director was only held accountable for delivering nine, not twelve, projects, and he got the additional team member he needed. If we hadn't gone through this exercise, he would have tried to complete all twelve with no additional resources and failed miserably.

It is vitally important that the project manager be proactive in controlling the project throughout its entire life.

---

"Though no one can
go back and make a
brand-new start, anyone
can start from now and
make a brand-new ending."

—Carl Bard

---

## MANAGE DISPUTE RESOLUTION

One of the things I have learned is that working with human beings means that some degree of conflict is unavoidable. Fortunately, following the process suggestions in this book will help greatly reduce tensions and misunderstandings on your projects. I was working with a client on a project in Silicon Valley, and we were in the middle of a planning session. Tension became high between two people on the team. Before I knew it, these two were really going after each other. They were verbally attacking each other, both were angry, and the situation seemed to be escalating even more. We called for a break and during that time I brought the two guys together to try to see if I could de-escalate the situation.

I asked, "So, George, what is the issue that you're having? Why are you angry?" Then I went to the other person. "Colin, what is your concern? What has you so upset?"

My goal was to understand each person's perspective so that I could articulate it to the other party and help them see the other's point of view. If neither was willing to budge from their stated position, the next step would have been to refer back to the charter document for clarification. If that still didn't resolve the issue, then I would have had to raise the issue to a sponsor and say, "We need help with this because George thinks we should go left, but Colin is just as sure we should go right. I need your help in resolving this."

## WHAT NOT TO DO

The project manager should be the voice of reason and the adult in the room. I have seen the project manager get just as angry as the two people yelling at each other, and that just worsens the situation. Now you've got three angry people yelling at each other, and that results in a total meltdown. The meeting usually ends prematurely, and it isn't resolved; it just percolates.

When intervening in a situation like this, it is important for the project manager to try to bring the points of view into the open. "Listen, we all work for the same company. If we don't succeed on this project, the company doesn't make money, and we all get hurt. So put your personal feelings for this person aside. Let's talk about moving forward. How do we do that? How do we advance this project? Let's figure out the right direction, and then you guys have to agree to go in that direction whether you personally believe in it or not."

An example of the other extreme is a project manager who hates conflict and tries to gloss over the incident because they want to avoid it at all costs. Their first reaction is to say, "Oh, there's no problem here. Let's just keep going" or "Let's table that for a later discussion." The problem is that the issue never truly gets resolved—the manager doesn't ever want to come back to it because they don't like conflict. So the issue festers, eventually ruptures, and blows your project up because you didn't address it. At PSI we want to address the elephant in the room right now before it gets any bigger. The longer it sits there and festers, the worse it gets, the more problems it will cause, and the harder it's going to be to fix.

Project managers who choose to ignore conflict within a project team also risk losing face because nobody wants to work for a project manager who isn't willing to take a stand. Team members expect the project manager to exert appropriate and professional control for the sake of keeping the project on track. Otherwise, a team member might think, "I don't believe this project manager is going to have the backbone to back me up and defend me if I need it so I better take care of myself." By comparison, once the team members realize you have their back, they'll run through a wall for you. They will probably do work on your project ahead of anybody else's project because they respect you and feel that you are supporting them.

## USING GROUP CONSENSUS

It's unrealistic to think that on a project team of twenty people all of them are going to agree on everything all of the time. While that would be ideal, it's simply not realistic. When the inevitable disagreement arises, you should aim for reaching group consensus instead. This is often misunderstood as a majority voting process. It is also sometimes incorrectly seen as reaching 100 percent agreement. Consensus means that a group reaches a point where the person in the strongest opposition can sincerely say something like, "Well, that would not be my choice, but I can live with it." Going back to the mountain climbing example I used earlier in the book: We all want to get to the top of the mountain, but different team members might favor different routes. Splitting up is not an option because the group has to arrive together. Harold might say that we should take path A, and Marjorie might insist that we take path B. Both people should have an opportunity to state their positions and be listened to respectfully. After this there should be an opportunity for the group to discuss both options and ask questions. When the group agrees to take path B based on whatever available metrics and information they have, Harold may still not agree, but he is willing to take path B to move the group forward. That's what group consensus means. We're going to move forward together despite our individual perspectives.

## HOW TO ENCOURAGE CONSENSUS

To encourage consensus you have to keep team members focused on the project goals, which means referring back to the charter. You engage with the members by asking, not telling. "Help me understand how taking route A supports this charter objective." Another asset you can leverage to help the group reach consensus is to bring your sponsor into the conversation. There are times when it might also be appropriate to bring in the internal customer to help the group reach consensus. For example, you might involve the customer if the conflict arises from *what* needs to be accomplished. On the other hand, if the conflict is regarding *how* to get there, it may be more appropriate to involve the sponsor.

## PREVENT CONFLICT EARLY ON

If you follow our process, the team writes the charter for the project as a group. If there is going to be conflict, this is where you want to have it happen so you can deal with it early in the process. Sometimes people are less rigid about their preferences when you address them as a part of charter formation. After you encourage everyone to come together on the same page and understand the project, the rest usually flows. Typically there's not really that much conflict after that.

I always tell people in the class if you talk to somebody who's been through the charter process before, and you ask them to describe the charter process in one word, they almost always say "painful." Why is it painful? It's painful because you're getting people in a room for three or four hours, locking the door, and saying, "We're not leaving this room until we all agree or come to some consensus on this thing." That's where the opinions come out and the verbal fisticuffs happen. But at the end of four hours, you unlock the door, and we're all going to move in the same direction. You might ask why we even do it if it is so painful. The reason you do it is because what makes it work is what makes it painful. You're getting all the conflict out in the first four hours of the project as opposed to having to fight these same battles over and over and over again for the whole life of the project.

# CHAPTER 7 KEY TAKEAWAYS

- Project managers must be willing and able to say no to the customer and/or senior management.

- It's better to negotiate a realistic schedule at the beginning of the project than disappoint the customer in the end.

- Careful attention needs to be paid to resolve the team member workload to avoid burnout.

- While it's normal for the project manager to be responsible for some activities, they must not take on too many tasks.

- Projects need to be prioritized. They cannot all be top priority.

- Some degree of conflict is inherent with any project team. Addressing conflict quickly and directly in a caring way can de-escalate the situation.

- By ignoring conflict or by pretending that it's no big deal, the project manager risks making it worse.

- Some project team conflict is predictable and therefore avoidable.

- Group consensus can be a powerful tool to move teams forward.

"The first responsibility of a leader is to define reality. The last is to say thank you. In between the two, the leader must become a servant and a debtor. That sums up the progress of an artful leader."

—Max De Pree

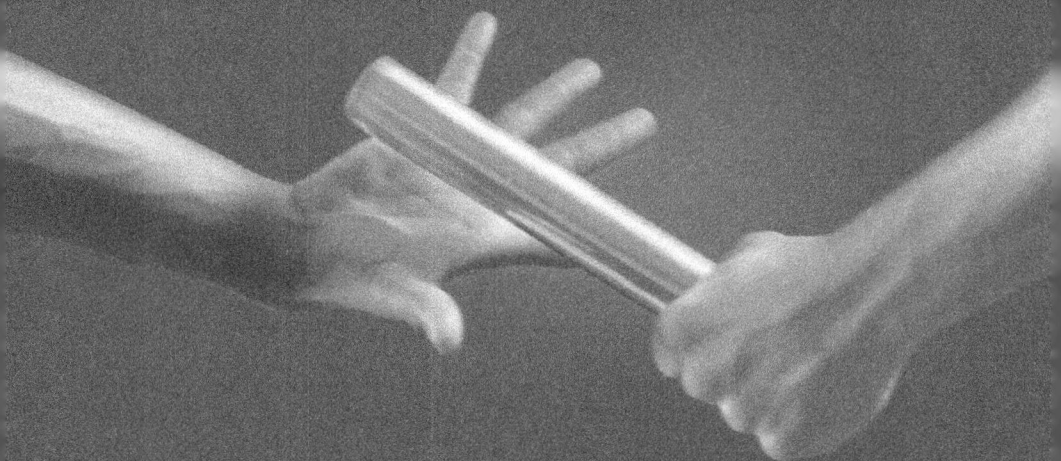

"Every great change is preceded by chaos."

—DEEPAK CHOPRA

# CHAPTER 8:

# SUPPORT PEOPLE
# WITHOUT MICROMANAGING

*A PROJECT MANAGER* who micromanages others runs the risk of derailing a project team through the excessive control exerted over them and their tasks. We work a lot with energy/utility companies across the United States. I recently taught a class for one of them where one of the participants in the class was a contractor who was brand new to the client but was very vocal in disagreeing with almost everything I said. While I always encourage participants to share their experiences, I hope they will have as open a mind as I do (often the disagreement is merely semantics, and we actually agree on the overall concept) but this person was "anti" everything. When I got to the point in the program where we were discussing project control, she proceeded to tell me I was making a huge mistake by allowing the team to have flexibility in their work.

Specifically, we were discussing the role slack or float plays in successfully managing a project. As we've discussed previously, in any project there are a set of activities in sequence from the start of the project to the end of the project that take the longest of any sequence of events in the entire project. If those activities are delayed by one day, your project is late by a day. If any one of those activities can be reduced by a day, then your project will save a day and you'll finish a day earlier. So, in order to finish your project on time, it is *critical* that those activities be accomplished exactly as planned. The good news is that critical path activities usually make up less than 10 percent of the activities in a project.

The other 90 percent of the activities in the project have what's called slack or float on them, which means those activities could be late by one, two, three, or four days, or sometimes six months, without holding up the end of the project. So we use that slack or float to identify which tasks can afford to be delayed and which have to be done exactly as planned. For example, if Nate has seventeen things on his to-do list for this week, we look at all of his tasks and say, "Well, how many of those can you realistically do?" and he says, "I can do three of the seventeen." In this case the three we definitely want to make sure get worked on first are the ones that are on the critical path, because if they're late, the project is late. Then we talk about the ones that are not currently on the critical path but have a very limited amount of slack/float such that if they were delayed by a day or two they would become critical. The remaining activities have a sufficient amount of slack that we can delay them until later, when he has more availability.

At least that's how it typically works. In the aforementioned class, the contractor said, "No, no, no. Every task has to be done exactly as the schedule says. It must start and finish exactly as scheduled."

We went around and around, and I kept saying, "But that's the whole point of slack. I mean, that's why you find the critical path of the project—we know that everything won't happen exactly as planned because that is not how life actually works. You might get sick or get called to jury duty or be tapped to solve an issue for a customer not related to the project. You can't force every single thing to fit into a box every single day."

Adamantly, she would not agree to this point. I kept digging deeper with her to try to understand why she was being so rigid and finally got the answer. She said that the only way that she knew how to be successful on a project was to make sure every single task happened (started and finished) just as the schedule said. After all, the schedule had the right completion date, so if every single task in the entire project was performed exactly as the schedule showed, then the project would finish on time. *She didn't understand the concept of the critical path.*

She was micromanaging. When you micromanage to the degree that you are dictating the specific start and finish dates for each and every task in the project, no matter what, it's obviously a nightmare for all involved. First of all, it's a nightmare for the team because your team members are not working on just that one project. They're also working on five other projects, and they're trying to focus on the highest priority for that day. Maybe their boss's boss just walked in and put something on their plate that's now the highest priority. But it's also a nightmare to manage a project that way because you're going to spend all of your time updating/massaging the plan as opposed to *managing* the plan. That's also the reason we don't want to go supergranular and plan tasks measured in hours or even a lot of one-day tasks.

## THE IMPACT OF MICROMANAGING

At PSI we try to keep everything in the range of five to ten working days—one to two weeks—for near-term activities (the tasks you know the most about). If you're an activity manager on six different project teams including mine, as long as I know that by Friday I'm going to get what I need from you, then I don't care if you did it on Monday and it sat around for four days, or if you stayed up all night Thursday night finishing it. As long as I got it on Friday as you promised, I am happy. So what is magical about five-to-ten-day tasks? It turns out combining micromanaging with short duration activities is a nightmare for all involved. In fact, the smallest duration we'll allow in a schedule is one day. Think about it for a moment. If you plan activities in hours, you are saying that it matters exactly what time of day a task finished. Now, does it really matter if the task was finished at 2:04 or 3:12 or 11:15? No! It only matters that it finished on Tuesday, not the exact time it finished. So we won't accept durations of less than one day, and we actually don't want many of those either. If you create a plan with a lot of one-day tasks, the schedule now shows task 1 has to happen on Monday, task 2 has to happen on Tuesday, and task 3 has to happen on Wednesday. All flexibility to do work in an environment where there's more than one thing going on at the same time has been removed. In project work, flexibility wins the day and improves the probability for success.

Our philosophy is to actively avoid micromanaging. Let people have the flexibility of a given one- or two-week period and they'll get the work done. Micromanaging a project team is an absolute disincentive. In the example I used earlier, I know that every time I go into this contractor's meeting, and one of my tasks is late because I didn't complete it on a specific day of the week, I'm going to get beat up and yelled at—even though it didn't matter because it didn't delay the project. Eventually, I'm not going to want to go to her meetings. I'm going to try to avoid her like the plague. Some people would say, "Well, then you make sure you do her task first so you can avoid the pain." But my experience has been that while some people will do that, more will think, "I'm just going to ignore her. She doesn't make any sense to me."

The impact is that the morale on the team is affected, and it's harder for her to manage that way because the more granular you get, the more tasks you have to identify. I might want one ten-day task in my schedule, and she might have twenty halfday tasks. As a result she has twenty times the number of activities I have. Where I might end up with a five hundred activity schedule; she ends up with a ten thousand activity schedule. Think about how much work that is to maintain and to manage. By the way, it turns out that the contractor didn't last very long with that energy company. She was gone within two weeks because her need to micromanage by overly controlling the work of others was in direct conflict to the company's team-centric project management culture.

## SUPPORT AND CHALLENGE WITHOUT MICROMANAGING

Project team members need challenge *and* support to stay productive. The trick is to be able to provide the oversight and support that people need without smothering them. When supporting people, there's an element of trust. It might sound something like, "Hey. What do you need from me? Are you having trouble in a certain area? Do you have too many things on your plate this week? If so, let's look at the schedule and see what could be moved to later."

> Project team members need challenge and support to stay productive.

Micromanaging is sitting in your office saying, "Hey. It's five o'clock. You need to be done already, and make sure tomorrow morning you do this, and by tomorrow afternoon you better have that done." Being supportive is asking, "How can I help?" and accepting that sometimes the answer is just to leave someone alone for a while.

In addition to support, providing an appropriate challenge is also a vital role of the project manager. You just need to know how and what to challenge on. There are many times when challenging is appropriate, but one that is overused is when somebody gives a duration for a task. Some people always want to challenge that right away by saying, "You shouldn't need that much time for that task. That's too long."

As I stated earlier in this book, we believe that the person whose name goes on the activity has to say, "That's my task. I own it." I can't put your name on the activity if you're not in the room. To further reinforce accountability, we have another rule that states that only the person whose name is assigned to an activity can give me its duration.

As you recall from Chapter 6, Jane and her boss, Bridgette, were initially at odds over the duration of Jane's task. The project manager respectfully challenged both individuals and eventually arrived at a compromise that Jane could commit to. It's important that Jane, and all activity managers for that matter, feels that she is being heard. It's about accountability and ownership. How can someone whose input was ignored be held accountable for a task? Similarly, how committed is someone to completing tasks in an environment where the project manager is constantly hovering over and hounding them? The answer to both is clearly "not much."

---

"Finding good players is easy. Getting them to play as a team is another story."

—Casey Stengel

---

# SANDBAGGERS AND OPTIMISTS

A question I get a lot is "Well, how do you handle people who sandbag?" *Sandbagging* is a term that means someone is going to downplay their ability to finish a specific task in a certain amount of time. Sandbaggers build in a safety net or buffer for how long it's going to take them to get a project task done. For example, they might look at a task and think that it will probably only be about eight actual hours of effort. In other words, if they did nothing but that one task, they would spend eight hours, or one day, of duration on it. But they work in a multiproject environment with lots of other things going on and competing for their time, plus they have their day job as well. So, to feel safe, they suggest a duration of five days, thereby giving themselves a buffer. They are sandbagging.

What's the big deal? So what if someone gives themselves a buffer of a few extra days? The problem is that durations become self-fulfilling prophecies. Those inflated durations that were "just in case" are always consumed. The buffer always gets used! But the real issue is the effect the buffer has on the project completion date. Let's say your project has 250 activities in it, which isn't a large plan by any means (we often work with plans that have two thousand or more activities), and 10 percent of them are on the critical path. If each of those twenty-five critical path items have been buffered by just two days, you've extended your project completion by fifty working days. That's two and a half months! That's why sandbagging is bad.

Project managers tend to worry a lot about sandbagging. It's one of the first things people talk about in our classes. However, our experience as a company, and certainly my experience personally in almost thirty years doing project management, is that it is much more likely that somebody will be overly aggressive or overly optimistic in their duration than sandbag. If somebody offers a duration of two days, I'll say, "Wow! Only two days. So, Martin, how are you going to get that done in just two days? Don't you have to … " and I'll start talking through the activity with them, and then it comes out that they're thinking sixteen hours of actual physical labor time, and I'll say, "Okay. So that's going to be done by Wednesday? Because today is Monday, you're going do it in two days."

They usually respond, "Well, no, I'm working on five other things."

I say, "Okay, you need to take that into account when determining your duration."

Martin responds, "Oh, then give me two weeks."

## WHY DO PEOPLE SANDBAG?

As a member of a project team, why would you sandbag? As previously discussed, you may want to create a safety net or buffer but it might also be a result of your previous experience with poorly run project teams where project management was punitive in nature rather than helpful—it was wielded as a club to inflict pain and place blame. Now when somebody says, "We're doing project management," you feel the anticipation of pain. You remember that your input was never solicited. They assigned you a duration and then harassed you when you didn't make the date that they gave you, but you never actually committed to that date. If they'd asked you, you would have been able to give them a much better date. But they didn't. And so, in your mind, you see project management as just additional structure used to harass people over deadlines.

Another reason people sandbag is for risk mitigation. They do it to give themselves a buffer in case the task doesn't go well, the unexpected happens, or uncontrolled circumstances are in play. In our classes we teach two alternative strategies for managing risk in a more constructive way. One way is adding activities to address the risk. Say you're developing a new product with five modules, and after each module is designed, it needs to be tested. You don't know on day one of the project which of those five modules is going to fail or how badly they'll fail, but history tells you, based on past experience with similar projects, you can expect two of them to fail.

So we address that risk by putting in an iteration of rework or debug to account for the fact that something's going to fail, and we'll need to address it. That's a risk mitigation strategy. We don't need to add a buffer to the duration now because we're going to call it out as a task called rework/debug. Which, by the way, is much more indicative of what's actually happening. Plus, if the rework/debug ends up not being needed, you can simply delete the extra tasks.

The other way to address risk is by adjusting the duration of *specific* activities. For example, what if you have a task that takes place outdoors? This particular task cannot be worked on if it's wet, which means the task is impacted by rain or other bad weather. You build in extra time for rainy days, basing your estimate on past weather data. That is not sandbagging. That's making the duration correct and accurate. By comparison, sandbagging is where you just give yourself an arbitrary buffer on all your tasks just to be safe.

## CHALLENGE APPROPRIATELY AND QUESTION ASSUMPTIONS

We will typically challenge duration estimates on the shorter side more than longer ones, unless they're just unrealistically long. Probably the most constructive time to challenge takes place once the plan's all put together. Let's say, for example, that you're looking at the critical path of the project, and you're four months beyond your deadline. The target deadline was December 31, but the plan shows you aren't going to finish until April 30 of the following year. You challenge the team by saying, "Listen, how can we do this differently? Can't we do those two things in parallel? What if we went out and hired a contractor? Could they come in and support you on that? Can that documentation task be outsourced?"

Another beneficial move the project manager can make is to take the lead on challenging assumptions. I remember working with a group diligently trying to compress their project to meet the target deadline. We'd been at it for an extended period and, initially, had made good progress but had now hit an impasse. One of the team members said, "We've done all we can. There's nothing left to compress."

After a brief pause, a different team member said, "I'm not sure that's true. We could solve the problem by adding a second production line."

Yet a third person responded with, "That would cost way too much. We will never get management to agree to that."

I said, "Let's not make that assumption yet. Let's try it and see what the schedule impact would be. Maybe we can make a case that management can agree to."

The cost for the new line was $150,000—not an insignificant sum, but it turned out adding this second line would save us two months on the project. Since the project was worth $400,000 per month in profit, spending $150,000 to earn $800,000 didn't seem like a bad idea at all!

Those are the kinds of challenges you should offer, but there are also some you should avoid. Never challenge somebody's intelligence or their work ethic publicly. Of course, it's perfectly acceptable to have a private meeting with a low-performing team member to ascertain what the issue is and how you can offer assistance. The most constructive challenges you can provide a project team are on their assumptions, pushing them to explore alternative, creative ways of resolving schedule issues and durations that are overly optimistic or clearly sandbagged.

Not all challenges have to come from the project manager. Effective project team members, working together, will challenge each other. They'll call out the sandbaggers and the overly optimistic people, and they'll say, "No. No. Come on. You always say twenty days, and you know for a fact it's only going to take you five. Be realistic."

Or someone will say, "There's no way you're doing that in three days. How are you defining the activity, because that's much more work than three days?" Then they talk through it together. And everyone has a better understanding in the end. Clarity is a beautiful thing! And so is a team that polices itself!

## MANAGING DETAIL-ORIENTED VERSUS BIG-PICTURE TEAM MEMBERS

I mentioned previously how, in our project management sessions, people in the same line of work or department will typically sit together because they all speak the same technical language and share the same perspective. I also said that project management should pull people down out of the clouds and up out of the weeds, putting them on the same plane to talk about the project in a way that accommodates both perspectives. To maximize your success, you need to have each individual on your team on the same plane, pursuing the same goal. They have different functions but a shared goal. Strategy is giving us direction, while sales and marketing are going out and talking to the customer, getting their preferences, feedback, and perspective. Engineering's job is to take this information and turn it into something you can actually touch, feel, build, and then sell.

To teach this point in our classes, we use a very simple exercise called the "Bake a Cake" project. The exercise starts off by asking the participants to identify the tasks required to bake a cake. I always play the role of project manager/head chef so I can drive us to the appropriate level of detail. I usually say, "Before we go any further, I know there are at least one or two people in the class right now thinking to themselves, 'This is easy—there's only one task. Bake the cake. Now let's all go home.'" Then I say, "And there are other people in the room who are shuddering at that thought because they're thinking, 'No, no, no. You need a hundred tasks—open drawer, remove spoon, inspect spoon for cleanliness, place spoon on counter, close drawer. Repeat seventy-five more times.'" This exercise never fails to show the participants that there are two very different approaches to planning, that effective project teams are always made up of people from both groups, *and* that you need a project manager who is going to balance the two.

The way that plays out in the real world is that there are some people who feel very comfortable managing a two-year project with twenty-four month-long activities. There are others on the team who think, "Okay, that's insane. For a two-year project you need twenty-four thousand activities." And the truth is, each one of those extremes will cause you to fail. If you really have twenty-four thousand activities in a two-year project, you're going to drown in the details. You're going to spend all your time as a project manager trying to keep the project plan up to date and managing the software tool instead of managing the project. Plus, I wouldn't want to be a team member on that project with one thousand tasks per month needing to be completed. As a result, you're going to fail because of excessive detail.

At the other extreme, you have a schedule with only a few long duration activities. Really big buckets of work are represented by tasks that are eighty or one hundred days long, and it's hard to tell what's really going on in those big buckets. What we find is if you take an eighty-day task and you actually break it down into five- and ten-day tasks, and you tie them together in the sequence of what happens first, what happens second, what happens third, they almost never equal eighty days. In fact, they almost never equal less than eighty days. It almost always ends up being ninety-seven days or 105 days instead of eighty days because the devil is in the details. You're going to fail again but this time because you did not have enough detail.

To build on an earlier example, a marketing person on the team is probably not going to care how many activities are in the plan. Because they are big picture oriented, they're going to say, "Based on my conversations with the customer, we need to have this feature set. And we need it by this date." They don't care about the detail. They just want to make sure you deliver all the functionality by the deadline. They'd be happy with four activities—design, build, test, deliver to customer. Of course, the engineering group is going to want all of the gory details.

Just like with Goldilocks and the three bears, we need to find the one that's "just right," but in our case the porridge is the duration, and "too hot" and "too cold" are replaced by "too long" and "too short."

## PROJECT TEAMS REQUIRE BOTH PERSPECTIVES

The truth is, we need both perspectives to be effective. Detail-oriented team members need that big-picture person to provide the proper direction and context. At the same time, the big-picture person needs detail-oriented people to bring a dose of reality and remind them what is possible without breaking the laws of physics. We need each other!

Normally by the end of our three-day planning session, we have a clear line of sight as to whether we can hit the target deadline for the project. Remember, this is the deadline we've been asked to meet, which we recorded in our charter and ignored during planning—at least until now. And if we cannot hit the deadline, we know why not. We understand what is holding us up. As a result, we either have the plan compressed back to meet the deadline, or we know why we can't make the deadline as currently established. In the latter case, we begin a dialogue with the internal customer to negotiate additional time, additional resources, or a reduction in scope.

If I have someone on the team who actually has to perform detailed work but is a high-level, big-picture thinker, what I do to pull that person down out of the clouds is to say, "Listen, I'm not asking you for one-day tasks. I really want things in the five- to ten-day range. But for you, I'll stick closer to ten days. If we take this forty-day task you have in your head, then what are the four ten-day chunks that we could use to lay this out? What would that look like?" The key is to ask them to explain exactly how they are going to do their work and then document it. They aren't really going to let forty days pass without doing anything, are they? Of course not, so what are they doing? What are the steps? If something is being shipped on a container ship and is scheduled to take two months (forty working days), are they going to just show up at the dock on the fortieth day and expect it to be there? No, they will have checked in periodically to make sure it's still going to arrive as planned. So let's build those check-in points into our plan. If ACME Corporations is building a piece of equipment for you that takes three months, rather than one ninety-day task, we'd push for more detail. We'd want activities like

"Confirm receipt of PO at ACME," "Confirm receipt of equipment 3D models," "Receive PPAP results," "Confirm ship date—first check," "Confirm ship date—second check," and so on. We don't want to add detail just to have more activities but to model how the work will actually be performed and to make sure the worry curve is shifted.

Alternatively, if I've got somebody who is giving me tasks that are only one or two days long, I'll say, "Can we take five of those one-day tasks and bundle them as one five-day task? Or can we take three of these one-day tasks and have one three-day task?" I tell them that it's perfectly acceptable for them to have a detailed checklist of things that need to be accomplished for each task. That checklist can be as detailed as they want, but we're going to include the task in our plan, not the checklist. So we try to take the super detail-oriented people and pull them up out of the weeds a little bit and guide them toward less granularity.

On both ends of that spectrum, you're trying to help team members think differently. How does an effective project manager do that? I think I have the answer for you. The most effective project managers are like the ones we have at PSI. They have the ability to see the big picture but also the ability to understand the details. They can see that if either one goes to an extreme, we're going to fail on the project. Most of us at PSI have technical or engineering backgrounds, so we can certainly get down into the weeds. We just don't let ourselves do it.

We understand the people who want to go into the weeds, but for a project team to be effective, we know we can't let them do that, and we're able to say, "Listen, I know what you're trying to do and I know why you're trying to do it, but trust me, you don't want to do that." And I always remind them if I let you have a hundred tasks that you could actually do in ten tasks, that's a hundred times I'm going to come back to you and say, "When did you start, and when did you finish? When did you start, and when did you finish? When did you start, and when did you finish?" For every one of these activities they list out, I'm coming to ask that question. Or they can have ten tasks, and I only have to ask ten times "When did you start, and when did you finish?" Which do they really want? Do they want ten or do they want a hundred? And I remind them that they can always have a checklist, separate from the project plan, that's as detailed or granular as they want.

> The challenge for many technical people is to flex beyond the math to be able to see the other side of project management—people.

All of a sudden they get it and say, "Ah, I want ten."

One powerful skill that makes you really effective as a project manager is being able to see the big picture while understanding how and where the details fit and helping the team members get to the "right" level of detail.

Since part of project management is process-oriented, this role commonly attracts engineers, IT staff, and other technical folks. Activity A takes five days followed by B, which takes ten days, followed by C, which takes five days. Total project duration equals twenty days. There's a math component to all of this, and you have to have the math-based skills to be effective. You have to be able to look at a project plan and say, "This doesn't make any sense. Something just doesn't seem right. These dates don't make sense to me." And you're able to dig into it because you understand the math part.

The challenge for many technical people is to flex beyond the math to be able to see the other side of project management—people. I know it's a bit stereotypical to say but my experience is that those of us who have really good math skills are often not the best communicators. You have to be able to understand the details but also understand where the project is going in the big picture and *how people will have to work together to get there.*

## COMMUNICATING EFFECTIVELY

Effective project managers have to be able to communicate with all of these types of people we are describing. Detailed versus big picture. Creative versus technical. Introverted versus extroverted. You almost have to be a translator. I've been in situations where two team members with opposing views are having a debate that eventually turns ugly. One side gets angry and says something about the other person that is pretty negative. I just smile and say, "I think what they're trying to say is … " and restate the argument in a less inflammatory way that hopefully helps to bridge the gap.

Another crucial aspect of communication within project teams is that you have to be comfortable talking to everyone. Each member on your project team has a preference of how they want to be spoken to. Some people you can speak to in a very straight-to-the-point way, and they're OK with that. In fact, they enjoy it. I spent six years in the navy, and the communication style was very direct, to say the least. I have to remember that just because that was my experience, and it worked OK for me, that doesn't mean that style will work for everyone on my team.

Knowing what motivates people is key. Some people like to be teased or joked with. Others don't. Some people appreciate being reminded of deadlines, while others may feel like that is nagging. Being aware of your own natural communication style and knowing the impact that it has on people is incredibly important. Knowing when to use a different approach is a learned skill and is especially important for keeping a project team moving in the right direction.

You've got to be able to talk that person off the cliff who's stressed out because they have an activity on the critical path that is going to be late. You have to say, "Listen. It's all right. It's OK. We're going to analyze the plan to see how we get that time back." There's no benefit in beating that person up about the bad news because they probably can't fix the issue, or they already would have. Use words like *we* instead of *you* or *I*. It's all about *we*. How are *we* going to get the three days back? I'm a big fan of being proactive, not reactive. Being reactive is berating a team member who is delivering bad news. Being proactive is taking that bad news, along with everyone else's update information—some of which is also bad news—analyzing the impact on the schedule, and then working as a team to remove the resulting slippage. When you're being a reactive project manager, you put yourself in the situation I mentioned in Chapter 4, in which the team member won't tell you there is a problem in order to avoid receiving abuse.

## COMMUNICATING FREQUENTLY

At a minimum you have to communicate on either a weekly or biweekly basis. This is driven by the necessity to make the needed course corrections to the project plan. We build a plan today that we believe is going to get us where we need to go, but by tomorrow that plan will need to change, because something will be different. Maybe somebody is sick or has been called to jury duty or perhaps we realize that we missed an activity. Since the project plan is static, we have to make periodic course corrections as we go.

I've already mentioned the analogy that says you're at the base of a mountain and you want to hike up to the peak. When you reach a part of the path that is washed out, you don't give up on your goal; you have to modify your plan and choose another route.

The same thing happens in organizational project management. We initially build a plan we think is going to get us to our goal, and then after one week (I'm referring to a weekly update cycle in this section, but having them every other week may be appropriate in longer projects) we come back and say, "Okay, we know what was supposed to happen—but what actually did happen? When did the task really start? When did it actually finish? Or what do we know today that we didn't know five days ago? What new tasks do we need to add to our plan? What durations do we need to modify? What did you realize was out of order? Do we need to change the sequence of certain tasks?" At the end of that session, you've updated the plan to reflect where you actually are at this exact moment in time. You've made it correct and accurate again.

During these updates something on the critical path has likely been delayed. You'll have to remove that slippage or lateness by compressing the plan again. But at the end of that update session your plan is back to being your best guess for the project right now, so that you will hit the date you promised. Then next week you repeat the process.

These weekly update meetings ideally involve people coming together in a room face-to-face.[10] As a project manager, you've sent them forms that remind them of the tasks they are currently supposed to be working on. Each activity manager completes the form with the actual status of each task. They then bring their completed forms (we refer to them as Activity Update Forms or AUFs) to the meeting and as a group you use these forms to update the project plan.

---

10  While I believe that face-to-face update meetings are ideal, the reality of working on global projects with geographically dispersed team members necessitates these meetings be conducted virtually.

It's also in your best interest as a project manager to prevent problems from arising in meetings. For example, prior to meetings I will often seek out forgetful team members and say, "Hey, remember that we have a status update meeting tomorrow? Are you ready? Do you have your activity update form already filled out?" While I often collect the update information "live" in the meeting, on larger projects I may take that information ahead of time. I'll give them a deadline to provide their forms to me, but realistically I can expect to get only about 80 percent of the forms back by the deadline. I have to chase the other 20 percent. Getting the information in advance saves time in the meeting, and, as the project manager, I avoid being surprised by status issues. Of course, this expediency comes at a price. I lose the dialogue about the activities and the challenge from other team members about completion dates. For instance, if I'm updating the project plan in real time, with the team all in attendance, either virtually or in person, and Frank tells me his task is complete, Logan has the opportunity to challenge that statement. Logan says, "Wait a minute, Frank. You told me when you were finished, I'd get X from you, but I haven't seen X." Frank then responds, "You're right, Logan. I forgot about that. I'm not done. I need three more days." When the update information is collected and entered prior to the meeting, this dialogue never takes place. Frank thinks he's done, and all Logan knows is that he hasn't received the thing he needs to start his task.

Clearly, these weekly, one hour or less update and control meetings serve two main purposes—modifying the plan to reflect reality and making the necessary course corrections, but they also serve as a way to facilitate conversations among the team members. In addition to these structured, planned conversations, there are other conversations that should happen every single day. As I am looking at the critical path of the project, I will check in with the people who are on the critical path to make sure that they have what they need to be successful. If a team member I've worked with in the past has been a problem for me, I'm going to reach out in a positive way and make sure that they're on the right track and have what they need. I don't want to micromanage, but I do want to provide support and challenge in equal measure. The Agile project manager method talks about daily stand-up meetings. While I don't believe it is necessary to bring everybody together again for a face-to-face meeting every single day (although it could be appropriate for certain shorter projects), you should absolutely be talking with individual team members and other stakeholders daily. Whether you have that stand-up meeting or not, as a project manager you are communicating with different people on your project team every single day.

# CHAPTER 8 KEY TAKEAWAYS

- Micromanaging project team members can have a detrimental impact on the effectiveness of any project team.

- Specific techniques are available to project team members to manage their tasks and allow flexibility without micromanaging.

- Effective project managers understand how to appropriately provide challenge *and* support for team members.

- There are predictable reasons for team members to either sandbag or underestimate durations, and project managers should work to address them.

- Effective project teams consist of big-picture people as well as detail-oriented people. Both are crucial, and effective project managers optimize the contributions of both while serving as a translator between them.

- The method and frequency of communication can significantly impact project team effectiveness.

- Face-to-face update meetings of one hour or less every week or every other week to make course corrections and the project plan correct and accurate are very important to keeping the team engaged and motivated.

"If everyone is moving forward together, then success takes care of itself."

**—HENRY FORD**

"The single biggest problem in communication is the illusion that it has taken place."

—GEORGE BERNARD SHAW

CHAPTER 9:

# COMMUNICATE LIKE A PERSON, NOT AN EMOJI

**SEVERAL YEARS AGO,** I was at a Microsoft partner conference, and the keynote speaker told a story about communication that surprised and amused me. The speaker spoke about his son, who had asked for help with writing a formal document. The father said, "No problem. What are you writing? Is it a letter? Is it an essay?" The son's response? "It's an email."

At first, the response struck me as really odd, but the longer I thought about it, the more it made sense. For a generation that's used to limiting their responses to 140 characters and has an attention span of seven seconds, one second less than that of a guppy, which is eight seconds, an email of a few hundred words may seem like a "formal" document.

Our declining ability to communicate well feels like death by one thousand cuts having come full circle. Initially, we communicated through pictures drawn on cave walls. Then, for generations, stories were passed down via spoken word. Eventually we developed written language and evolved into sharing the written word. Huge novels such as *Gone with The Wind* (418,000 words) of 1936, *Atlas Shrugged* (645,000 words) of 1957, *Mission Earth* (1.2 million words) of 1985, and *Marienbad My Love* (2.5 million words) of 2008 were published. At that point, written communication was in its heyday. Then email came along (in 1972 but not mainstreamed until the late eighties and early nineties with the advent of the internet) and the slow descent began. Emojis were created in Japan in the late nineties, and Twitter came along in 2006. It seems everyone is seeking to communicate in as few words as possible and using pictures to accomplish that—emojis and communicating in pictures have become a way of life. Today, everyone communicates like the caveman—in pictures. Even the most popular project management software allows the use of smiley faces and frowny faces as a communications tool. The problem with returning to picture-based communication and using the fewest words possible to communicate is that it actually leads to a breakdown in communication.

Just look at this case study. At 9:00 a.m. on a Wednesday in July 2020, Taylor Baxter, vice president of international operations for Century Manufacturing Company, an Atlanta-based corporation, calls a meeting. He says, "Folks, the executive committee has approved the new plant in Buenos Aires, and it's up to us to get it running. I don't think I have to tell you how strategically important it is that we open this plant as quickly as possible and that we get it right the first time. To gain a foothold in the Argentine market against established competition, we've got to maximize the surprise factor, and the plant has to produce world-class quality from day one. The executive committee has directed that the new plant open for operation in fourteen weeks; that's seventy working days. Our total project budget is $6 million. I think if we make this our top priority, we won't have any difficulty meeting these targets. Any questions?"

Surprised by the announcement and concerned about how such a big operation will finish in just fourteen weeks, Corporate Maintenance Manager Victor Schmidt raises his hand and says, "Maybe we should develop a plan for this project, so we know exactly what has to be done and who will do what, when."

As a project champion, Taylor feels the vague outline of the project that he's given is enough to get his team started, so he replies by saying, "We don't have time for that, Vic. This isn't rocket science! We open plants all the time. This is just a simple startup for a small facility in a leased building. I think we all know what has to be done, so we better get busy. I want to see some real teamwork on this one. If any questions or problems come up along the way, just let me know."

So the team gets to work. Victor heads to the Buenos Aires plant and the rest of the team starts doing what they *assume* Taylor wants. On day fifty, Victor calls Martina Karlsson, industrial engineer at the Atlanta plant and says, "The contractor is here to install the electrical system. They brought the equipment layout you sent them. Unfortunately, the floor plans you based the layout on don't look anything like the space we've leased here. The floor space on your layout is about fifty percent more than what we actually have."

Martina is frazzled, but she isn't surprised by what Victor has to say. Several weeks earlier when Taylor had flown to Buenos Aires to check on the project and visit company plants in Rio and Caracas, he was supposed to ask the Buenos Aires property landlord for the floor plan so he could deliver it to Martina, but he had forgotten. Martina called the landlord to get the plans, but it took a while for them to go through. When Martina finally got the plans, she assumed they were incorrect—the space seemed suspiciously large—but she didn't check with Taylor. He'd recently left for Missouri to attend to an ill family member and, since he was a vice president and she wasn't, Martina didn't want to bother him when he was away from the office with her question. To solve the problem without Taylor, Martina decides to get a flight the next evening and sort out the issue. Electrically, nothing else can be done until Martina arrives. The electricians remain on the clock being paid, waiting for Martina.

On day sixty-eight, two days before the project deadline, Adrian Guerro, Buenos Aires plant manager, calls Taylor at the Atlanta office. It's 4:45 p.m., nearly closing time, in Atlanta.

"Taylor," Adrian says, "we have a problem. Rafael Moreno arrived this afternoon to teach the standard ten-day training program for our new personnel, but we can't find the raw materials he usually uses during the training course. I started to call purchasing about it, but I don't know who requisitioned our initial supply of materials or what delivery date was specified."

Taylor is very irritated by this unwelcome news and immediately begins to search for the person responsible for the problem. Upon reflection, he realizes he has no one to blame but himself. He *assumed* Martina would do the ordering even though it's not a responsibility that is typically hers. "I'll call the manager at our Caracas plant and have him ship you enough materials to get through the training," he says. "They're not exactly like the materials your plant uses, but they're the closest we have in South America. In the meantime, I'll rush an order of the new materials. We're already running late and over budget due to the layout fiasco!"

Adrian knows the materials won't arrive from Caracas for at least a few days—a problem since twenty-five new employees are slated to arrive the next day for the training. Adrian agrees to ask Rafael to busy the new employees with personnel policies such as benefits, salaries, and safety rules. However, he doesn't think these topics will occupy enough training time, so the company may have to pay the new employees to sit at home while the training materials are in transit, wasting precious time and money. Not only will the company lose more money, but the delay and lack of organization are frustrating Rafael and other Buenos Aires staff. Not exactly a great start to new business relationships in Buenos Aires.

This is the situation Taylor, who told his team when they started the project that he wanted to see good teamwork, has led his team into. The problem is that while Taylor talks about teamwork, *he doesn't do anything to build it.* Saying you're on the same team, whether it's in sports or in business, doesn't mean a thing unless that group of people learns to work together.

When I was a kid, I played youth baseball on the Phillips Shoes team. The first day of practice, we all got shirts and hats that said Phillips Shoes. We looked like a team, but looks can be deceiving. In the beginning, half of us didn't know which inning we were in, and almost none of us ever communicated with each other on the field.

Although we looked like a team, we weren't a team because, other than shouting the occasional, "We want a pitcher, not a belly itcher," we didn't know how to work together. At least not yet.

A similar disconnect occurred during the Century Manufacturing Company project. Everyone had the same badge and the same logo on their shirt, but they weren't accountable to each other, they didn't communicate with one another, and they weren't a team.

Now, if Taylor had listened to Victor and agreed to have the Century Manufacturing Company project team meet face-to-face for three days to plan the project, not only would they have had a clear project direction, but they also would have developed a sense of accountability to each other. "Order startup materials" would have been identified as a task in the plan and would have a clear owner—there would have been no confusion. If Taylor had actually fostered teamwork among his team, rather than merely paying it lip service, Martina and Victor would have been better able to deal with the issues while he was out. Perhaps they could have proactively solved the layout issue before it cost the project time and money.

One of the fundamental components to successful teamwork is communication. If you can't talk to your team, you can't be successful. The key to developing communication is face-to-face, eyeball-to-eyeball communication. Project managers have to facilitate this type of communication. They also have to invite communication. Phrases such as "This isn't rocket science," "We do this all the time," and "If any questions come up along the way, let me know" don't invite any critical participation from the team. In fact, they deter team members from voicing any concerns because they all recognize that the further removed you are from a project, the easier the work seems. Our three-day planning process forces communication by getting people in a room together at the very beginning of the project to talk about the project and share their opinions about it.

Project managers need to recognize that while projects are obviously undertaken for the customer, their success or failure falls squarely on the shoulders of the people on the team. The people matter the most because they are the ones who have the ability to deliver the project. Here's how you can avoid letting emojis and technology derail your team communications.

## HAVE TWO-WAY CONVERSATIONS, NOT ONE-WAY COMMUNICATION

A fundamental underpinning of the Project Success Method is to get people out of their silos. We as human beings love to get stuff off our plate or crossed off our to-do list. That desire leads to one-way communications like email or text or a quick post on a "collaboration" tool like Jira. I'm not sure it's conscious, but I think deep down they know that if they call this person to have a conversation, they might learn that they are not really done. While an actual conversation may uncover a deficit or lead to more work on their part, an email or text about a topic checks the box—so it's no longer their concern. Now it's on someone else's plate. I firmly believe this deep-seated desire to check the box leads to the "throw-it-over-the-fence mentality" that is a major reason projects fail.

Technology is great for a lot of things, but when you communicate in pictures or by using the fewest words possible, you create unclear communications. When you send an email or text, there's no dialogue—instead, you have a series of one-way communications. This makes it virtually impossible to discuss any complex issues that are happening within a project, and it opens the communication up to misinterpretation. Be honest, how many times have you misinterpreted the tone of an email or a static document? The only way to manage a project effectively is to develop the project around clear two-way conversations. One-way communications should only be used for simple, clear questions that have yes/no answers or are used to piggyback on conversations. In other words, it's okay to text or email questions before a conversation takes place or follow-up responses afterward. Conversations need not be the only form of communication, but they are the most important by far.

## NEVER ASSUME

When PSI updates project plans, we send out a form that people use to write their start and finish dates on and send it back electronically. At least, that's what used to happen with project updates. Today, people return those plans with a smiley face, checkmarks, a frowny face, arrows, or an "OK." These forms are supposed to let me know the status of their tasks, but what does a smiley face mean? Does it mean you're happy that the task is finished? Does it mean you're in a good mood? Does it mean ha-ha, you're never actually going to do this task, I just don't know it yet? Does the checkmark mean you're done, or that it's on your checklist of items to complete eventually? These picture communications are confusing and encourage the recipient to make assumptions  about their meaning. As a project manager, if I assume a smiley face means that someone has finished their task when it actually means they're happy with their progress and plan to get to it next week, the project is delayed, and I don't even realize it. If I pick up the phone, someone can say, "I'm on time" or "I'm late," two or three words that are substantially clearer than a smiley face, but still not enough. I need to know *when* they're going to be done.

Verbally telling me when you're going to be done is commitment. Sending a smiley face isn't.

Project work is black and white. You want to be as clear as possible. Gray is the enemy. The more we rely on emojis, pictures, and the like, the more our communications are open to interpretation and the more gray areas we create.

## COMMUNICATE OVER THE COURSE OF A PROJECT

One of the reasons the Project Success Method works is that it forces communication over the life of a project. This happens for two reasons. One, the project manager plans update sessions on a regular basis. During these sessions, the plans are updated, and everyone is aware of what's happening, what issues have come up, and where the project stands. Two, every team member knows the project manager has their back. They know they won't be penalized for not getting something done on time. As we saw in Chapter 7, they know the project manager can take bad news without flinging it back in their face, and they know that the team—not the individual—will be responsible for making up any slack. This drives their accountability to get it done.

## APPRECIATE TECHNOLOGY, VALUE PEOPLE

Many project managers approach communication from a technical standpoint because they want software to be the answer. Can we use email to communicate? Of course. Everyone on the team can receive an electronic form that they can fill out electronically and email back to their project manager, but is this the most effective way to communicate? No, because software isn't the answer; it's a tool.

Say a project manager, Carol, sits with the team during a control meeting. Anne tells Carol that she's finished her activity; however, when Carol goes to update it as complete, Chris says, "Hold on, Anne, I'm not really sure you're down with it. I thought you said that when you were done, I would get the study results. I haven't seen those, so I'm not really sure you're done."

Anne says, "Sorry, Chris. I totally forgot about the study results. You're right. I'm not done. Carol, I need three more days."

Electronically, that conversation would never happen. Anne would mark her activity as done, but Chris would never start on his activity because he wouldn't have received the data he needed. He would keep waiting for Anne to finish her activity and provide the results he needs. In this case, the update would get to Carol without her having any idea that her project was about to run significantly behind schedule.

Technically, project communications can happen electronically, but if you choose technology over people, your project won't be successful. While your communications will be fast, you'll sacrifice quality, clarity, accountability, and, ultimately, project success.

## PUTTING IT ALL TOGETHER

Everything we've talked about so far in *How Teams Triumph* is really about communication. Viewing people as your biggest asset; gathering the right team; making people matter; working with your team to plan for unknowns; exercising project control; and supporting people without micromanaging are all about communication. Now that we have the foundation for how to communicate effectively as a project manager, let's take a look how failing to do any one of these things can lead to a communication breakdown and, subsequently, a poor project outcome.

---

Slippage is like compound interest:
The longer it sits there, the bigger it gets.

---

## CASE STUDY: ATHENS PLANT SILVER ANNIVERSARY CELEBRATION

Once again, we visit Century Manufacturing Company, only this time a plant team is planning a silver anniversary. A week before the event, Plant Manager Dale Greco stops by the office of Human Resources Manager Tracy St. James.

It's 6:15 p.m., and Dale is surprised to find Tracy at her desk. When Dale asks Tracy how many people to expect for the celebration, Tracy says, "The current count is one hundred and three. I don't think it will change much between now and next Saturday."

"Only one hundred and three?" Dale asks. "That's a real disappointment! That doesn't sound like the event I'd envisioned."

"I guess it all depends on which 'vision' you're talking about, Dale," Tracy says. "When you first asked me to handle this event, you described it as a 'family affair'—an opportunity for the Athens plant family to have some fun, eat some good food, and celebrate our twenty-five successful years as a team. This business of running a fundraising effort for Children's Hospital, inviting the general public to participate, and trying to attract media coverage was not part of your original vision. If it had been, I would have asked for more time, a larger budget, and several people to work with me on this project."

Dale responds, "Speaking of the media, are any of the local television stations planning to send a camera crew?

"Frankly, Dale, I haven't made much of an effort to get television coverage," Tracy says. "Based on my estimates, we'll just about break even on this event—which, incidentally, was our original financial goal. I don't think you want television coverage of you presenting the administrator of the Children's Hospital with a check for one hundred dollars. Dale, if I had known what you wanted from the beginning, I could have made this a fabulous success for all involved. As it is, I'm just trying to get through it with minimum damage to our public relations."

So how did Dale and Tracy get into this situation? One obvious issue is that the scope of the project has clearly changed, something commonly referred to as scope creep. What Dale originally asked Tracy to do and what he's now expecting are totally different. Dale changed the scope of the project from an internal company event to what he hoped would be a media extravaganza and fundraiser. Additionally, there is a severe lack of communication. Finding out only a week before the event that he's not getting the event he desired is too late. It's too late to fix any issues. It's clear that Tracy knew Dale had a change in vision at some point during the planning process; however, once Tracy understood that change, she apparently continued working on her tasks as if Dale's vision hadn't changed at all. She should have had a conversation with Dale about the changed vision and shared her frustration. And Dale should have been checking in regularly about the progress being made. Sadly, even when they finally did have the conversation, Dale failed to acknowledge Tracy's concerns, instead asking about the media attendance. Conversations are only helpful if the involved parties actually listen!

In this case study, the worst possible scenario occurs because at the end of the project no one's happy. Few people plan on attending, those who are won't have a good time since that's no longer the goal, and media coverage, which is suddenly the focus, is unlikely to happen.

Lack of communication contributed to the two issues that derailed this project. If Dale had developed a clear vision and had had a conversation with Tracy when that vision changed to confirm that she was bought-in, there would have been a much higher probability of success. If Tracy had raised her concerns when she first learned of the change in direction, the project could have succeeded. If Dale and Tracy had communicated on a regular basis, this situation never would have occurred.

---

## "BUT THE HOOD WAS UP!"

Scope creep occurs when the scope of the project increases as the project progresses. You take on more and more that you didn't agree to initially. So, if the original scope of a project was to build a bread box, but by the end of the project you've built a bread box and the two-story house that goes around it, you've experienced scope creep.

When I do trainings, I often ask who is typically responsible for scope creep. Most people say the customer, upper management, senior management, or leadership. This group definitely can be responsible for scope creep, but there's another group of people who are just as responsible for scope creep. That group is the team. When a team member creates scope creep, it's far more dangerous to the project than when a customer creates scope creep, for two reasons. One, the customer is paying for the product. They have every right to ask for a change to the scope as long as the project manager has every right to say, "No problem, we need three more weeks, and it's going to cost another thirty thousand dollars." That negotiation has to happen. Two, customer-driven scope creep tends to be well documented, and everyone on the team knows it. But if a team member changes the scope, they tend to do it on the fly, they don't document it, and the change isn't publicized. Their heart is always in the right place; their intent is not nefarious. They genuinely believe it's the right thing to do. They think, "This project is finally going to give me a chance to fix that *other* issue, which has been a problem for years. It won't take long and will provide benefits to future projects." The problem is that fixing that other issue is of absolutely no value to the customer of *this* project! What if you dropped your car off at the dealer for an oil change and were handed a bill for $1,000 when you picked it up? You look at the bill and notice that they flushed the radiator and replaced the fluid, replaced the spark plugs and wires, changed all the belts and filters in addition to changing the oil. Would you be happy? Of course not! You look at the service person and say, "What is all this? I just wanted an oil change!"

And they reply, "Oh, the hood was up, so we took advantage of that to take care of these other things too. You were going to need those done eventually."

You look at them in disbelief and yell, "No, I didn't! I'm selling the car. I was never going to get any of that done!"

Well that's exactly what you're doing to your customer when you add unauthorized scope—when a team member makes what he or she believes to be a very important change to the project, there's no discussion about it, and no money or time is allocated to do it. When a team member does those things, they are literally stealing time and/or budget to do the thing they've changed. Think about what happens if every person on a project creates a little scope creep—it creates a significant amount of work that has to be done and will likely cause the project to finish late or go over budget.

---

"Be brave enough to start a conversation that matters."

—Margaret Wheatley

# CHAPTER 9 KEY TAKEAWAYS

- Communicating with pictures (emojis), short responses, or not communicating enough with a team in a timely manner is ineffective, leads to communication breakdowns, and, ultimately, project failure.

- Project managers can avoid communication breakdowns by:

  ○ Having two-way conversations

  ○ Never assuming that a vague communication means one thing or another, but rather asking the messenger to clarify

  ○ Communicating over the course of the project

  ○ Appreciating technology, but valuing people

- Communication is the foundation of project management.

- Scope creep can completely derail a project.

- The most dangerous scope creep occurs when a team member changes the scope of a project without letting anyone know, thereby using time and money for that creep that wasn't allocated for that activity.

- Project managers need to recognize that projects are not about the project manager or the customer. They're about the people on the team.

"One good conversation
can shift the direction
of change forever."

**—LINDA LAMBERT**

"The difference between face-to-face conversation and any other medium of communication is simple: no distractions allowed."

—ALEXANDRA PETRI

CHAPTER 10:

# USE A GLOBAL MANAGEMENT MINDSET

*ONE COMMON MISCONCEPTION* is that traditional project management approaches do not work very well globally because of problems with language, cultural nuances, or time zone differences. The Project Success Method bridges gaps across international organizations. It works well because it draws on proven principles and focuses on the human element of project management. PSM is not done any differently in international scenarios, but the benefits of PSM are perhaps even greater, as it helps overcome some of the unique dynamics presented by globally dispersed project teams.

A typical project with which we could be involved might have design control in the midwestern United States, with parts being manufactured globally (including in Brazil, China, France, and the United States), and final assembly in China. So we're working one project in four very different time zones and four very different cultures. How is managing a project that also includes cultural differences different than managing domestic projects? In reality the two aren't all that different, especially if the domestic project crosses several time zones and states. If you have a team on the East Coast, West Coast, and in the South, you can't walk down the hall and talk to a team member. The same is true if you're working with an international team. Communication, accountability, and teamwork are crucial for all projects both domestic and international. However, there are a few things that you might run into with an overseas project, such as language barriers, that you won't find in a domestic project.

Because the majority of our clients at PSI are US-based multinational companies, our perspective uses that lens. On the plus side, the team members are used to doing business in English and have considerable exposure to Western culture and norms. However, we need to be particularly sensitive to the non-US team members to make sure we consider their preferences, customs, and time zones while doing this work. For example, we'll often rotate the time of our update and control sessions so that they are not always during the workday in the United States and the middle of the night in the other locations. We prefer to share the pain, and it ends up truly feeling like a real team effort—not one dominated by a single country.

## THE INCREASED IMPORTANCE OF FACE-TO-FACE CONTACT

When it comes to long, complex, or global projects, we have found that getting the project team in the same room at the beginning of a project has an incredibly positive impact. This is core to all of our projects, but it is even more true for international work. When you have team members face-to-face for the initial planning session, many of the cultural issues are minimized or alleviated because the people involved in the project are forced to leave their silos and form relationships with their team members. When you opt out of having those initial planning sessions, and the team is spread across countries, barriers such as distance, language, culture, and politics are that much more difficult to overcome.

As I've mentioned several times, people like their silos. They like being around others who speak their language, be that literal or figurative, think the way they think, and share their values. The issue with international projects is that they create more silos. Even if you and I speak the same technical language, if you're in the United States, and I'm in China, the fact that we're not in the same time zone gives me one more reason not to talk to you. When people are twelve hours apart, there's never a good time to talk because someone will always have to stay up late or get up early to talk to the other person. That's problematic. So the nature of international work creates just one more barrier that allows us to stay in our silos. It's one thing to be in an office together in a matrix. It's another thing to be in different countries in a matrix. At least with a domestic matrix, you have the possibility of walking down a hallway to speak to a team member. You can't do that when half of your team is in China and half of them is in the United States.

> Our solution to forcing team members out of their silos is to get everyone in the same room.

Our solution to forcing team members out of their silos is to get everyone in the same room. We do it with US-based projects, and we do it with international projects. We bring the entire team together for the initial planning session, where we write the charter and complete the network diagram as well as the first compression session—all within three days. During that time, not only does the project get planned, but the team starts acting like a team. People start relating to each other and fostering relationships, just like they do in the United States. After that initial planning session, everyone goes back to their respective countries, but each person is no longer an email address—they're a person—and their bond with their teammates is much stronger. This leads to more engagement and accountability among the team.

The barrier to entry in getting everyone in the same room is cost. No matter which company we are working with, when we first suggest getting an international team together in one room for a planning session, the response is always "Are you serious? You want me to fly ten people from China to the United States? Do you have any idea what that will cost?"

When projects are planned via email or Zoom, it creates a lot of confusion and significantly lengthens the time needed to plan. One part of the team thinks they're going left, while the other part of the team thinks they're going right. Some team members feel left out completely and disenfranchised from the very beginning. In the end, you have individuals working at cross purposes as opposed to a team pulling in the same direction.

When we are involved on global projects, our clients are willing to make the investment to bring everyone on the project team together *physically*. It is a crucial step in any project team's success. In that three- to five-day period team members come to know each other as more than just an avatar as they build *their* plan for *their* project—the one they can commit to and be accountable to.

Then for the remainder of the project, whether it's twelve, eighteen, or twenty-four months, the work can be done virtually. But that initial planning session has to be done together, face-to-face. If the mentality is "We can't incur that cost," then frankly they're not going to be successful. The management's mentality should be "We're willing to make the investment to bring everyone together at the start of the project because that investment will be recouped many times over by the end of the project." Suppose the cost to bring the team together (fly the team members from the United States and Brazil to China) is $50,000. Is that money well spent? It really depends on how much the project is worth to us. I have seen projects where a single month of delay would lose the company $400,000 in profit—not revenue, but profit. Another project had liquidated damages in the contract of $1 million for each day the project was late. Would

> "Coming together is a beginning. Keeping together is progress. Working together is success."
>
> —Henry Ford

you invest $50,000 to avoid losing $400,000, $1 million, or even more? I know I would. Those travel costs are a drop in the bucket to ensure an on-time, successful project.

Another thing to think about when considering a $50,000 or other initial cost is, what if being late isn't an option? If a major global sponsor of a worldwide sporting event such as the Olympics or FIFA World Cup misses the start date by a month, they're sunk. The games are over. The matches are over. I bet they would wish they had spent $50,000 to not be late.

I remember going to Kiev, Ukraine, in 2012 to observe a quarter-final match of the UEFA Euro. As I was walking toward the stadium, I noticed a brand spanking new Sheraton hotel that was adjacent to the stadium. I thought to myself, "What a great location. They must be raking in the revenue." As I continued into the stadium, I realized that the hotel wasn't open! It was scheduled to open June 1 but still wasn't open on the twenty-first, when I attended the match. You can't tell me that management didn't wish they'd spent a little bit of money up front to make sure that the hotel opened before the matches started.

## CULTURAL ISSUES AND HOW TO MANAGE THEM

Going into an international project with awareness that there might be differences in culture, language, and company culture is critical. Here are a few tips for managing language barriers, work expectations, differences in company culture, titles, team participation, and scheduling.

### LANGUAGE

Finding a common language is the most obvious barrier when working on an international team. When you have team members who speak Portuguese, Chinese, and English, how do you find a common language? Translators are helpful, of course, but even if everyone knows English, that doesn't mean you'll be on the same page linguistically.

I learned this the hard way once while working on an international project. Initially, the planning process went really well. The whole team went to the planning session and we completed a few updates without any real crises. During the third update, it became clear that the project was slipping by three days, so I said to the group, "Listen, guys, this is unacceptable. We have to fix this if we can."

Immediately, someone stood up and said, "Stop. That's a very offensive thing you just said."

I had no idea what that person was talking about. Eventually, I discovered that in that country the use of *unacceptable* is offensive. I was stunned. Never in my life had I thought *unacceptable* would offend anyone. Needless to say, regardless of the country or countries you travel to, you must be mindful of the words, phrases, or terms you use.

Even though I sometimes say things that don't translate, the Project Success Method creates a common language among every team I've worked with. While terms for design, engineering, or project management may differ, after that initial face-to-face planning meeting, everyone knows what the project scope is, why it's important, and what they need to do to help deliver the project on time.

Sometimes, the literal translation isn't correct, so don't make assumptions. One of my coworkers worked in Mexico for several years, and he has an interesting story about the use of the word "mañana." Like me, he believed mañana meant "tomorrow." So, when someone on his project team in Mexico said that they would do a task mañana, he expected it the next day. When the next day rolled around, and the task remained undone, my colleague reminded his coworker about the task and was again told mañana. This went on for several days. Finally, he discussed the issue with a different Mexican colleague, who explained to him that in their culture mañana was not a promise of tomorrow—it just meant "not today." Once my colleague understood that, he readjusted his expectations and was able to work more effectively.

In Japan, I learned that when someone says *hai*, which is somewhat similar to "yes" in English, and nods, they aren't actually saying yes. Instead they're saying, "I've heard what you've said, I understand what's been said, but I'm not committing to anything." That's a vastly different meaning than what I expected. I thought it meant "Yes, I'll do that." Culturally, the Japanese don't want to offend other people. So, while saying *hai* doesn't mean they've agreed to something, saying, "That will be difficult" essentially translates to "That is never going to happen." Clearly, having local language context is helpful. In these two examples, a friend on the project team forewarned. If you are not as fortunate, you should be aware of the potential pitfalls and proactively seek out clarifications.

Sometimes the way words are used varies so much that native speakers of the same language have trouble communicating with each other.

I grew up in South Carolina, where we have a popular dance called the shag. The shag is a partner dance done primarily to beach music from the fifties and sixties. One day, I went to a comedy show in Myrtle Beach that featured a British comedian. He said, "I was at a club here in Myrtle Beach, and this girl comes up to me and says, 'Do you want to shag?' I thought, 'What a country.' I was extremely disappointed to learn that she was only asking me to dance." In England, *shagging* doesn't mean dancing. It's slang for sex, which goes to show that sometimes even people who speak the same language don't really speak the same language.

The final thing I'll mention with language and translation is, there is a distinct difference between conversational English and technical terms. I've been in several situations where the translator is absolutely stumped by the words we use, how we phrase things, or how quickly we speak. As you can imagine, this can cause a whole host of problems. Consequently, it pays to select a translator with the requisite skills for the assignment at hand.

## COMPANY CULTURE

Sometimes, members of an international team might not understand the company culture their foreign counterparts operate under, which can cause problems.

Once, I flew to Japan to help a client plan a project. At the beginning of our three days together, I started explaining our process to the team, which comprised two different branches of the company. Things were going well—the conversation was open, everyone in the room was participating—until the general manager of the company walked in. Since I don't speak Japanese, our conversation went through a simultaneous translation. With a simultaneous translation, an on-site translator sits in a booth with headphones on and translates what I'm saying to everyone else; they are listening through headphones in real time. Well, when the GM entered the room, someone explained that he needed a microphone in order for the conversation to be translated. The GM looked at the person, his face turning red, and he proceeded to read that person the riot act. I later learned that the GM was mad because he thought people were making decisions without him, and he certainly didn't feel his conversation about it needed to be shared with me. In addition, he didn't want people from two different branches of his company talking. Apparently, there was bad blood between the groups, and the GM was afraid his employees were "airing dirty laundry." We lost about half a day of planning because we had to let that situation settle before progressing with project planning. That was a huge cultural issue we had never encountered before.

When it comes to international project management, you simply never know what kind of internal company politics you're going to step into. Just know that they may arise, and when they do, it may delay your planning process.

## PARTICIPATION

Another nuance is that the most senior person in the room typically does most, if not all, of the talking, and it's really difficult to get the junior people, the ones actually doing the work, to say anything while "the boss" is in the room. If the senior leader is not going to be a member of the project team, we typically invite him or her to join and kick off the session and give some direction but then leave before the planning begins so that the more junior participants feel comfortable speaking up. (By the way, this happens, albeit to a lesser extent, in the United States as well. If the senior vice president or some other senior leader is in the room, it has a chilling effect on open dialogue from the project team. No one is willing to discuss existing issues when their boss's boss is in the room.) Something I learned on my most recent project in Japan is how much Japanese team members dislike feeling unprepared for a planning session. Even when told, "We'll develop the content together next week," they have premeetings so they can walk in with "the answer." Otherwise, they would be very much out of their comfort zone.

## TITLES

In many cultures titles are very important and have specific meanings. I remember having to change the title of our activity manager and project manager roles to activity lead and project lead in one country because the title of "manager" connoted higher pay. This is not as true in the United States.

## WORKING HOURS AND WORK EXPECTATIONS

Another interesting aspect of cultural consideration is what it means to be on time. In some cultures participants are in seats and ready to go fifteen minutes before the session starts. In fact, in Japan and parts of Europe, you can set your watch by the train schedule because punctuality is so important. In other cultures, being on time isn't held in such high esteem; starting fifteen or twenty minutes late is considered normal/acceptable, and one never starts until everyone has coffee.

Speaking of coffee, I was working on a project in Brazil a few years ago, and one of my colleagues on the client side (an expat from Western Europe) was lamenting his inability to get the team to work through lunch, or at least to eat quickly. Having worked on a half dozen projects in Brazil, I understood exactly where he was coming from. In many cultures, the food consumed during the meal is secondary. It's more about spending time with your friends and connecting with them. In Brazil the concept of getting coffee "to go" is unheard of—one consumes it at the point of purchase, usually while talking with a friend. And this can actually take place on the way back from lunch! The point is, that aspect of that culture is important to Brazilians, and we must not attempt to change it. We just need to understand it so we can work around it.

Another issue with working hours, which I hear about more than I see, is agreeing on what it means to show up on time and work a full day. Culturally, workers in some countries are used to showing up late, and no one minds. It's the way business is done. That, of course, is not how we do it in the United States.

## CALENDARS

When you look at the calendar for the project, pay attention to each country's holidays, as the time of year holidays are celebrated, and the duration of those celebrations vary widely from country to country. In China during the Chinese New Year, for instance, no one works. If you have suppliers in China or design work being done in China, don't count on any of it getting done until Chinese New Year, which is tied to the lunar calendar rather than the Gregorian calendar, is over. In France and other parts of Europe, it's customary for the whole country to virtually shut down during an entire month in the summer.

Normally, getting everyone in the same room for a planning session gets rid of any calendar surprises; however, there was a one-off event that temporarily put a kink in our planning of the London Olympics.

We finished the plan, compressed it back to meet the deadline, congratulated each other on a job well done, and returned to our respective countries. A few weeks later, I got a call from the project manager. She said, "Can you help remind me how to put in a holiday in the project calendar?"

I said, "What did we miss?"

She said, "We didn't miss it. It's a one-off, but it's the royal wedding."

When a British royal weds, it's a national holiday, and the entire country shuts down. No one works, and nothing is open, yet it never occurred to me to even ask about a national day off for a wedding. Now when I ask everyone to bring their country's holiday calendar, I specifically ask if there are any one-time events we need to consider that might affect the project delivery date.

## CUSTOMS/LOGISTICS

Customs vary so widely from country to country that it would be impossible to explain the differences between each; however, one similarity they share is that they can cause issues if they're not planned for.

I recall a project in China that specified parts would be made in China with production to take place in the United States. Well, not long after the parts had failed to arrive to the United States, the project manager started doing some digging. It turned out that the failure to make the parts rested with the customs process, not the Chinese supplier. The tooling needed to make the parts had been shipped from the United States to China several months before; however, it was seized by customs, and no one had been notified.

Another example: In 2018 we were teaching one of our courses in Israel. Well, our materials got held up in customs. When we asked what the problem was, customs informed us that the issue was with the pens in one of the boxes. The pens were four-colored BIC pens that were used on some of our exercises. After a lot of discussion, they eventually released our other materials, but they would not give those pens back, and they never told us why. This was particularly baffling because the trainer, who had put a similar pen in his checked bag, got through customs with the pen just fine. The lesson here is, learn to plan for the uncertainty of customs. What will you do if materials are held up in customs?

---

## DON'T REINVENT THE WHEEL

It takes years of immersion to fully understand a culture. Instead of trying to figure everything out on your own, find someone from the country you will be working in—this could be your client—and spend thirty to forty-five minutes talking with them about cultural differences that could affect the project. You might include these questions:

- What cultural missteps should I watch for?

- Which words, phrases, and gestures should I avoid?

- Is there a certain dress code I need to adhere to?

It helps if the person you've asked to speak with has some knowledge of the United States and how American companies operate. This type of person will have a better understanding of where you might clash with their own culture than one who isn't overly familiar with how American corporations operate.

---

## LACK OF SUPPORT FROM ABOVE

Senior management support is crucial, and expectations must be honest and transparent. A great example of a lack of support was a project we helped out with in eastern China. At the end of a full week of chartering and planning, where the testing requirements were clearly defined in the charter on day one, the team had built a schedule that met the project requirements and deadlines—or so we thought. After a very difficult day of compression, we noticed one of the engineers quietly get on the phone and then come back to say that testing time was *triple* what he had articulated earlier in the week. Clearly, the customer had started the week not believing that the supplier could actually deliver and, when we developed a plan showing they could, the customer simply changed the requirements to protect the existing supplier. The engineer acknowledged that the "new" testing requirements would not be mandated for an existing supplier. The facility at the time was a joint venture between a United States and a Japanese company. A year or two later, the partnership was dissolved, and we always wondered whether thwarted improvement efforts such as this project were a deciding factor.

There is a lot written about doing business internationally: building relationships, understanding what common behaviors may be considered rude in another country, and avoiding business and social missteps. While these are important, we repeatedly discover that they take a back seat to the culture that develops from a successful project team. Working with local/foreign teams of US-based companies, there is an acceptance or tolerance of behaviors that would perhaps otherwise be a problem in trying to make a sale or close a deal. I am sure we have all unknowingly done something in another country that would be considered rude. But I am also sure that the local team understood completely that there was no rude intent on our part.

## REDUCING LANGUAGE CHALLENGES

Most of the clients we work with are US-based multinational companies for whom English is their business language. In reality, in any of these global projects, there is a very wide range of spoken English among project team members. As a result, we make it a priority to keep charters, plans, and all related written communications simple and consistent. Where English is a second language, many understand written communications more easily and quickly than verbal communications. This works out well because updates and control rely more heavily on written communications than verbal. Paying careful attention to this structured approach keeps people engaged and minimizes the number of team members who might go silent or limit their engagement because they are not as comfortable speaking English.

This doesn't mean that there is less need for face-to-face communications where English is a second language—quite the opposite because otherwise team members might use the language barrier as an excuse to operate within a silo. Most people operating in a native-language environment are still absorbing communications through osmosis, even if they are not paying full attention. Alternatively, those operating in a second-language environment miss nearly 100 percent of the communications if they are not focused and attentive, especially if the speaker is not in the room but is instead participating remotely.

There are other advantages of face-to-face meetings with second-language team members:

- They reduce the number of people multitasking during meetings. For example, if someone is working on email during a conference call conducted in a second language, little or nothing is understood or retained from verbal communications.

- They provide meeting facilitators with an enhanced ability to manage distractions.

- The facilitator can monitor and react to engagement and comprehension by team members much more easily.

## CHAPTER 10 KEY TAKEAWAYS

- Face-to-face contact for all team members on any project team is critical. It is even more important when working with teams across nationalities and languages.

- Cultural issues related to language, working hours, politics (external and internal), customs, job titles, participation expectations, and calendars can affect project outcomes.

- Language issues should be anticipated and accommodated at the outset of a project. This is true even for US-based multinational organizations for whom English is their official language.

- Spending thirty to forty-five minutes speaking with someone who knows the nuances of these challenges can save you from making critical missteps.

- Written communications become even more important with team members working in their nondominant language.

"Once you understand and appreciate other people's cultural backgrounds, then you can also connect with them more"

**—ANONYMOUS**

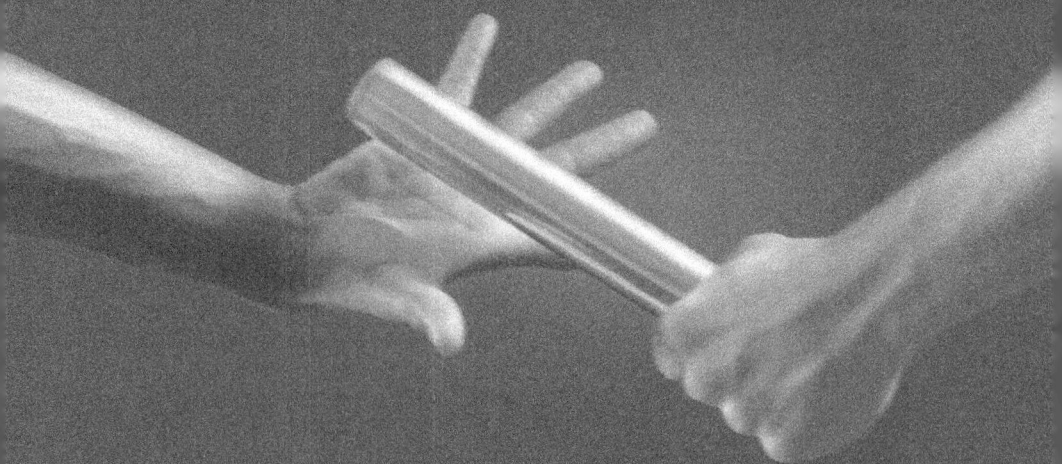

# HOW YOUR TEAM
# WILL TRIUMPH

*IN 2009 PSI* went to work with a Fortune 1000 engineering company. The company was successful, but there was some concern around project management. Every project manager did things their own way, so nothing was uniform, and the results showed it. The CEO didn't want to require that his project managers use the Project Success Method, but he recognized overall project performance needed to improve. So he decided to fund their project management initiatives, including travel costs, for three years. The three company divisions were given the options of bringing in PSI for training only, engaging with PSI for training and consulting/mentoring, or electing to do something else, but they had to do something.

Because this organization was so fact driven, they had data going back to 1983 that showed how they had performed on each and every project. As it turns out, they killed many of their projects before the final product was developed. Unfortunately, by the time most projects had been killed, the company had used most if not all the time and resources allocated to that project, so they had overspent, overused the resources, and still didn't have a product they could put out. The projects that actually got finished were nine months late.

The worst-performing division in the company elected to go all in. Their business unit VP said, "We'll take all the help you can give us." Over a three-year period, we trained everybody on his team and worked with them side by side to plan their projects. Three years later they had gone from being the worst-performing division in the company to the best. And that VP is now the CEO of a different semiconductor company.

Over that three-year period, they tracked their PSM projects and compared them to the non-PSM projects in the other two divisions. While the non-PSM projects continued to perform as they had previously, they found that *PSM projects were only 0.9 months late on average and reduced overall cycle time.* That's a huge savings in personnel costs alone. Imagine the cost of paying fifteen or twenty California-based engineers to keep working on a late project for an additional 8.1 months. They were also able to recognize projects that were not going to be successful and kill them early, usually within the first few weeks after planning. So, to summarize, the division was able to kill bad projects early, reduce overall cycle time, and reduce lateness by 90 percent. I'd call that a victory.

This is just one example (of many) that shows how the Project Success Method can help businesses operate more efficiently with predictable results.

In a matrix environment, project managers have little or no direct control over their project team members, but they have complete control over how they choose to work with those individuals. Project managers who truly build teams by developing strong relationships and trust within those teams deliver quality projects on time and within budget.

As a project manager, for your team to triumph, you first have to build your team. This requires developing the communication skills that encourage team members to respect each other, talk to each other, and understand what each person needs to do to get the job done. It also requires accepting a new model of project management, one that replaces punitive, static project management that doesn't listen to people and relies heavily on software with one that understands that people are the greatest asset.

After working on thousands of multimillion-dollar projects, PSI has developed a project management method that does just that. By gathering the right team, ensuring people matter, making your team accountable, planning for known and unknown challenges, letting team members set their own durations that can change if needed, and developing a relationship with team members that encourages openness, you can build high-quality, actionable project plans that your team will be committed to delivering.

When you get people in a room, force them out of their silos, and use conversation as your foundation, you will start building a team. After all, project planning should always be about people first and process second.

> Project planning should always be about people first and process second.

One of the coolest things about the Project Success Method is that you get to see a group of people become an actual team over the course of three-to-five days. Whenever teams sit down for their first planning session, they gravitate to their silos. Marketing sits with marketing, and engineering sits with engineering, but by the end of these sessions, there are no silos. Someone from marketing will be having coffee with someone from engineering, and everyone will be slapping hands and hugging once the planning process leads to a deadline that's on time and on budget.

We don't promise to create miracles, and we're probably not going to invent the successor to the internet, but if you do the things I've outlined in *How Teams Triumph*, you'll find problems much earlier, have time to fix them, and have the information needed at the beginning of the project to reset customer expectations or have the information needed to cancel the project before it wastes time and money.

Don't let your team be like that Georgia Tech team that got me and Joe talking about teamwork in 2017. Don't let their shoulders slump, their motivation wane, or their interest in supporting the rest of the team fall by the wayside. Teamwork is everything. You as a project manager have to be the person who motivates, encourages, and builds that team.

Now that you've read this book, take what we've done, understand it, and try to implement some of the processes and techniques we've talked about, because I know you can be successful doing this. The Project Success Method works. Treating your team with trust works. We teach it. You need to live it.

# GLOSSARY

**ACTIVITY:** Any time-consuming element of a project plan with identifiable beginning and ending points that contributes directly to the production of project deliverables.

**ACTIVITY MANAGER:** A member of the project team who has responsibility for managing execution of an activity in accordance with the project plan including quality specifications, scheduled start and completion, and budgeted cost. This person "owns" the activity's duration estimates and predecessor choices.

**AGILE METHODOLOGY:** Refers to a group of software development methodologies (including Scrum) based on iterative development, where requirements and solutions evolve through collaboration between self-organizing cross-functional teams.

**BACKLOG:** A list of all things that need to be done in a project under a Scrum framework. Includes technical requirements as well as product feature and functionality requirements known as "user stories."

**COMMUNICATION:** The activity of imparting or exchanging information such as facts, ideas, thoughts, feelings, observations, and opinions. May be conveyed through speech, writing, behavior, signals, and visuals.

**COMPRESSION:** The reduction of the planned duration for an activity or project.

**CONVERSATION:** Dialogue, typically informal, between two or more individuals to exchange ideas, thoughts, or feelings.

**CORE TEAM:** Group brought together (often as appointed by management) in the early stages of a project to begin development of project definition and plans. Typically represent all involved functional areas and possess broad knowledge of project business and technical requirements.

**CRITICAL ACTIVITY:** Any activity along any critical path in a project.

**CRITICAL PATH:** A connected series of activities whose combined duration is the longest of any path through a project.

**CRITICAL TASK:** See "Critical Activity."

**EXTERNAL CUSTOMER:** The person/group outside an organization for whom a project is performed/delivered.

**GANTT CHART:** A graphical schedule in bar chart format.

**GROUP CONSENSUS:** Decision-making or resolution by a collective rather than by an individual. Members agree to support the decision as being most representative, or in the best interest of, the group even if it does not perfectly align with or reflect their individual perspective.

**IN THE WEEDS:** A common English-language idiom; it reflects an individual working or focused at such a low level that they become overwhelmed by requirements and lose sight of overall, big-picture objectives.

**INTERNAL CUSTOMER:** The person/group within an organization for whom a project is performed/delivered and who usually funds the project.

**KNOWN UNKNOWN:** A condition or circumstance that exists or can be foreseen but cannot presently be quantified or measured; an assumption that cannot presently be validated. Can often be handled proactively in planning projects.

**MATRIX OR MATRIX ORGANIZATION:** Entity with an established hierarchal structure among formal groups (such as functional areas, departments, or product lines) but with a secondary reporting structure for projects and members of project teams.

**NETWORK DIAGRAM:** A graphical project representation showing the activities of the project and the precedence relationships among the activities.

**PAPER SCHEDULE:** A common English-language idiom; it reflects a timeline that presents well visually but was created in the absence of an underlying plan and thus may have no basis in fact.

**PREDECESSOR:** Activity whose start/finish is required before a subsequent activity can start/finish.

**PROJECT CHARTER:** A "word picture" that broadly but clearly defines quality expectations and other key attributes of the project at a given time.

**PROJECT MANAGER:** The person with overall responsibility for leading the project team through the planning and controlled execution of a project.

**RESOURCE:** Any entity that contributes to the accomplishment of project activities; most commonly used for staff (human resources) but can be equipment or materials as well. Often referred to as the "physical labor" to get the job done.

**RESOURCE HISTOGRAM:** Time-scaled display depicting the quantity of an entity required (typically staff) per time period. Histograms usually also reflect resource availability so that periods of overload (where resource requirements exceed availability) can be readily identified.

**SANDBAGGING:** A common English-language idiom; it reflects a strategy of downplaying or misrepresenting capabilities in order to lower expectations. May be done in an attempt to simply lighten workload or to create a scenario where performance can then exceed anticipated results.

**SCOPE CREEP:** Uncontrolled changes to the intended work content of a project (scope changes not properly managed by the team). Typically reflects an expansion of customer requirements or the addition of project deliverables without accounting for corresponding impacts to project budget or schedule.

**SCRUM:** An Agile methodology framework for planning and executing projects (most commonly in software development) through short development and testing cycles called "Sprints." The contents in terms of development requirements for individual Sprints are typically identified by the team and are not extensively planned upfront.

**SLIPPAGE:** Gradual and cumulative negative deviations in project progress versus schedule or in project cost against budget.

**SPRINT:** A development and testing cycle (typically two-to-four weeks' duration) under Scrum. The work content for each Sprint is identified and self-managed by the team.

**STAKEHOLDER:** Any person/organization that can significantly impact or be impacted by the results of a project, especially including the customer/client, project sponsor, project manager, and activity managers.

**SUCCESSOR:** Activity that has a start/finish directly linked to the required start/finish of an earlier activity.

**TASK:** See "Activity."

**TASK OWNER:** See "Activity Manager."

**UNKNOWN UNKNOWN:** An unforeseen (surprise) condition or circumstance that will be handled reactively in managing projects.

**UPDATE AND CONTROL MEETING:** Formal session to update actual and anticipated project performance (time, cost, and quality) against the plan to identify deviations and execute corrective action.

**VALIDATION:** The action of checking a plan to confirm that it comprehensively and accurately captures project requirements.

**WATERFALL PROJECT MANAGEMENT:** The "traditional" model of planning and executing projects through a linear and sequential organization of phases and deliverables.

**WORK BREAKDOWN STRUCTURE (WBS):** A logical hierarchy of work packages involved in a project.

www.ingramcontent.com/pod-product-compliance
Lightning Source LLC
Chambersburg PA
CBHW031504180326
41458CB00044B/6691/J